MW00699752

PRE-CALCULUS

Author:	Robert A. Sadler, Ph.D.
Editor:	Mary Dieterich
Proofreader:	April Albert

COPYRIGHT © 2019 Mark Twain Media, Inc.

ISBN 978-1-62223-767-8

Printing No. CD-405033

Mark Twain Media, Inc., Publishers
Distributed by Carson-Dellosa Publishing Company, Inc.

Visit us at www.carsondellosa.com

Table of Contents

Table of Contents (cont.)

Introduction: To the Teacher

Mathematics is one of the most diverse subjects that a student will encounter in public school. To some people it is a language, to others it is an art, and to still others it can be a science. To one person it might be a useful and productive tool, while to another it could be an engaging and entertaining game. It can be a study in itself, a window to the complex technology of our modern age, or a key to the understanding of some of the most intriguing and elegant aspects of nature.

It is, perhaps, unfortunate that we often encounter mathematics in a set of somewhat isolated courses, each dealing with a particular facet of the discipline. From this experience, we often conclude that each area of mathematics is a separate endeavor, with only a marginal connection to the others. We would regard as intolerable an English curriculum that featured a course in nouns, followed by another in verbs, and so on, but we accept, without question, a view of mathematics that is just as fragmented.

Some math courses, however, force us to embrace several areas of mathematics. Calculus is one of them. An applied problem (word problem) in calculus can sometimes involve logic (when the problem is analyzed), geometry (when diagrams are drawn or spatial relations are recognized), elements of algebra (when the problem is being set up), calculus (differentiation or integration), algebraic manipulation (when results of the calculus operations are reduced to simpler terms), and even graphing (when the results are converted to a visual image). It would be advantageous to encounter a unifying course before the rigors of calculus are approached. Fortunately, there is such a course—pre-calculus.

Pre-calculus attempts to provide an overview of the skills in algebra, functions, trigonometry, analytic geometry, and graphical analysis that are often thought to be crucial to success in calculus. It also attempts to construct a bridge to calculus by providing some introductory insight into sequences and series.

Lesson One: Algebra Fundamentals—A Review

Angela was mystified. She was reading a computer manual and noticed that a computer stores whole numbers in a different way than it stores numbers with decimal points and fractional parts. "What's the difference?" she exclaimed to her older sister. "Numbers are numbers, aren't they?"

Her sister was taking a calculus class in her senior year of high school. She patiently explained to Angela that there were several types of numbers, including the familiar counting numbers that we use to count the number of volleyball players on a court or the number of cows in a field and the rational numbers that we often use to express measurements of distance, weight, or temperature. She said that Angela would learn more about different types of numbers in the math classes that she would take in her next two years in school.

NUMBER SYSTEMS

Like Angela, we are sometimes tempted to say that numbers are all just numbers and lump them all into one big category. In reality, however, there are several number systems whose properties are different from one another. Although we often use these different types of numbers, we seldom stop to think about them. Throughout this book, and later in calculus, you will need to use several types of numbers and recognize their properties.

Numbers can be classified as cardinal numbers, ordinal numbers, or nominal numbers. **Cardinal numbers** are numbers that are used to indicate how many objects are in a group, a collection, or a set. (See the next section for a discussion of sets). For example, there are nine players on the field in a baseball game and 12 objects in a dozen. Nine and 12 are used here as cardinal numbers.

Ordinal numbers are numbers that indicate the order of objects in a group, a collection, or a set. We often think of these numbers as positions in a line or finishing places in a contest, and we usually express them as **first, second, third,** etc., instead of **one, two, three,** etc. In some cases, however, both forms are used. For example, "Central High School took **first** place in the state basketball tournament," or "Central High School was number **one** in the state basketball tournament."

Nominal numbers are used to identify a person, place, or thing. The number address on a house, the number on a credit card, or the number on a football player's uniform are nominal numbers.

There are other ways of classifying numbers, however, that are of more interest in calculus and other areas of higher mathematics.

Lesson One: Algebra Fundamentals—A Review (cont.)

NATURAL NUMBERS (COUNTING NUMBERS)

The first numbers that we usually learn are the **counting numbers**, or **natural numbers**. Intuitively, we know that the counting numbers start at 1 and extend upward, in steps of 1, to an indefinitely large quantity. They are easier to describe, however, in terms of a **set**. In mathematics, a set is just a collection of objects. Each of the objects is called an **element** or a **member** of the set. Sets are sometimes described as a list of the members, separated by commas, and enclosed in "curly braces", {, and }. In this notation, the natural numbers can be expressed as follows:

{1, 2, 3, 4, 5, ...}

where the three dots, ..., can be read as "and so on." Note that the set of natural numbers does not contain zero or any negative numbers.

WHOLE NUMBERS

The set of natural numbers plus the number zero is the set of **whole numbers**. The whole numbers are described in set notation below:

{0, 1, 2, 3, 4, ...}

We sometimes say that the natural numbers are a **subset** of the whole numbers. A set, **X**, is said to be a subset of another set, **Y**, if and only if all of the elements of **X** are also elements of **Y**. As you can see, all of the members of the set of natural numbers, **{1, 2, 3, 4, 5, ...}** are also members of the set of whole numbers, **{0, 1, 2, 3, 4,...}**.

INTEGERS

Integers are sometimes called signed numbers. They include the set of whole numbers and the negatives of the natural numbers. Their description in set notation is shown below.

{..., -3, -2, -1, 0, 1, 2, 3, ...}

The **positive integers** are just the set of natural numbers, **{1, 2, 3, 4, 5, ...}**. The positive integers are therefore a subset of the integers. They are also a subset of the whole numbers and of the natural numbers. The **negative integers** are the set **{...-5, -4, -3, -2, -1}** that represent quantities that are less than zero. The minus sign, of course, indicates that these quantities are negative. The negative integers are a subset of the integers. The zero no longer represents nothing, but, instead, indicates the middle number of the system. The integers are often represented by the number line shown below.

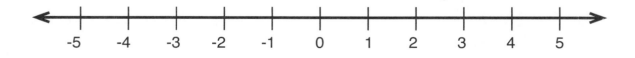

Integers are used to represent quantities that have no fractional parts but can have positive or negative values. Golf scores (above and below par) and temperatures (rounded to the nearest degree) are examples of quantities that can be represented by integers.

Lesson One: Algebra Fundamentals—A Review (cont.)

The **absolute value** of an integer is its distance from zero in either the positive or negative direction. Therefore, the absolute value of an integer is just its numerical magnitude, without its sign. The absolute value of an integer is denoted by a pair of vertical lines on either side of the integer.

$$| 6 | = 6 \qquad | {-5} | = 5 \qquad | {-27} | = 27 \qquad | 195 | = 195$$

$$y = 16,\ | y | = 16 \qquad x = -1357,\ | x | = 1357$$

RATIONAL NUMBERS

A **rational number** is one that can be written in a fractional form, **a/b**, where **a** and **b** are integers. The set of natural numbers, the set of whole numbers, and the set of integers are subsets of the set of rational numbers.

Rational numbers can be converted into decimal forms by simply dividing the denominator into the numerator. For example:

$$\frac{5}{4} = 1.25$$

The decimal form of the number will either **terminate**, as shown in the example above, or result in a **repeating decimal** as shown below:

$$\frac{8}{3} = 2.6666666 \ldots \qquad \frac{2}{7} = 0.285714285714 \ldots$$

IRRATIONAL NUMBERS

Some numbers must be expressed as decimal quantities that neither repeat nor terminate. These numbers are called **irrational numbers**. Some familiar examples are shown below:

$$\sqrt{2} = 1.41421 + \text{more}$$

$$\sqrt{3} = 1.73205 + \text{more}$$

$$\pi = 3.14159 + \text{more}$$

Irrational numbers can be either positive or negative. An important property of irrational numbers is that they **cannot** be represented as an integer divided by another integer.

Lesson One: Algebra Fundamentals—A Review (cont.)

REAL NUMBERS

The set of **real numbers** includes all of the rational numbers plus all of the irrational numbers. There are an infinite number of real numbers, and there are an infinite number of real numbers between any two real numbers. The sets of natural numbers, whole numbers, integers, and irrational numbers are all subsets of the set of real numbers.

Real numbers are often plotted on a real number line, like the one shown below. Unlike the integers, real numbers are **dense** along the line. An infinite number of real numbers can be plotted between any two real numbers.

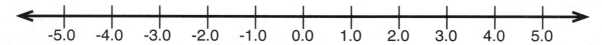

The concept of absolute value is defined for real numbers and rational numbers in the same way as for integers.

| 57.95 | = 57.95 | -139.46 | = 139.46

COMPLEX NUMBERS

There is one more class of numbers that is of interest to students who plan to take calculus. **Complex numbers** are the most general numbers that are encountered in algebra. They are expressed as **a + bi**, where **a** and **b** are real numbers, and **i** is the square root of **-1**. The **bi** term represents an imaginary number, the square root of a negative quantity. The **a** part of the number is often called the **real part** and the **bi** part is called the **imaginary part**. Complex numbers are often assigned to variable names as follows:

$$x = 45.25 - 15.87i \qquad y = 6.8 + 5.9i$$

Complex numbers are often the solutions to quadratic equations (see Lesson 5) of a certain type. They are used, for example, in physics, electrical engineering, and communications theory to represent the concept of phase in a wave.

Two properties of complex numbers that are of interest are the **complex conjugate** and the **modulus**. The **complex conjugate** of complex numbers is the number with the sign of the imaginary part reversed. If a complex number is assigned to a variable name, the complex conjugate is denoted as the variable name followed by an asterisk, *.

$$x = 10.7 + 5.9i \qquad x^* = 10.7 - 5.9i$$

The **modulus** of a complex number is analogous to the absolute value of a real number. It is the square root of the sum of the squares of the real and imaginary parts of the complex number.

$$x = 6.6 - 3.7i \qquad |x| = \sqrt{6.6^2 + 3.7^2}$$

$$y = 8.9 + 9.2i \qquad |y| = \sqrt{8.9^2 + 9.2^2}$$

Lesson One: Algebra Fundamentals—A Review (cont.)

Complex numbers must be plotted on a two-dimensional graph like the one shown below. Two complex numbers, **a** and **b**, are shown plotted. Their complex conjugates and modulus representations are also shown. Note that the imaginary part is plotted on the vertical axis and the real part is plotted on the horizontal axis.

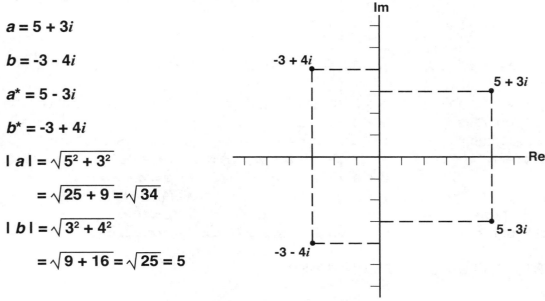

$$a = 5 + 3i$$

$$b = -3 - 4i$$

$$a^* = 5 - 3i$$

$$b^* = -3 + 4i$$

$$|a| = \sqrt{5^2 + 3^2}$$

$$= \sqrt{25 + 9} = \sqrt{34}$$

$$|b| = \sqrt{3^2 + 4^2}$$

$$= \sqrt{9 + 16} = \sqrt{25} = 5$$

The real numbers are a subset of the complex numbers. In fact, the complex numbers can be thought of as the set of all real numbers and imaginary numbers. The diagram below shows how the other numbers are all subsets of the complex numbers.

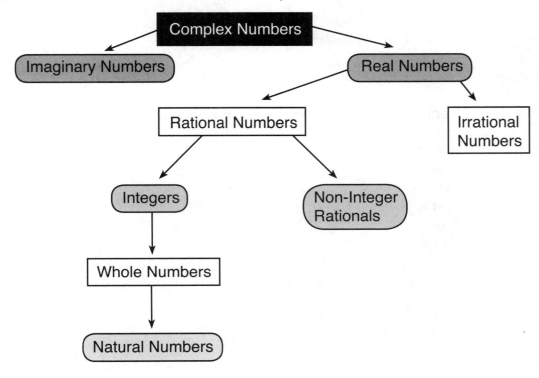

Lesson One: Algebra Fundamentals—A Review (cont.)

PROPERTIES OF THE REAL NUMBERS

You are probably already familiar with the properties of the real numbers. The table below is included as a review.

Real Number Properties

For real numbers *a, b, c*	Addition	Multiplication
Closure Properties	$a + b$ is a real number	$a \cdot b$ is a real number
Commutative Properties	$a + b = b + a$	$a \cdot b = b \cdot a$
Associative Properties	$(a + b) + c = a + (b + c)$	$(a \cdot b) \cdot c = a \cdot (b \cdot c)$
Distributive Property	$a \cdot (b + c) = a \cdot b + a \cdot c$	
Identity Properties	$0 + a = a + 0 = a$	$1 \cdot a = a \cdot 1 = a$
Inverse Properties	$a + (-a) = 0$	$a \cdot (1/a) = 1$ ($a \neq 0$)
Multiplication Property		$0 \cdot a = 0$
Zero-Product Property	If $a \cdot b = 0$, then $a = 0$, $b = 0$, or $a = b = 0$	

SOME OPERATIONS ON COMPLEX NUMBERS

Complex numbers must be manipulated differently than real numbers. The rules for addition, subtraction, multiplication, and division of complex quantities are shown below.

Addition

$$(a + bi) + (c + di) = (a + c) + (b + d)i$$

Example:

$$(5.6 + 3.4i) + (3.9 + 4.2i) = (5.6 + 3.9) + (3.4 + 4.2)i$$
$$= 9.5 + 7.6i$$

Subtraction

$$(a + bi) - (c + di) = (a - c) + (b - d)i$$

Example:

$$(3.5 + 4.7i) - (2.4 - 3.2i) = (3.5 - 2.4) + (4.7 - -3.2)i$$
$$= 1.1 + 7.9i$$

Lesson One: Algebra Fundamentals—A Review (cont.)

Multiplication

$$(a + bi) \cdot (c + di) = (a \cdot c - b \cdot d) + (a \cdot d + b \cdot c)i$$

Example:

$$(2.2 + 3.1i) \cdot (4.5 - 1.5i) = (9.9 - -4.65) + (-3.3 + 13.95)i$$
$$= 14.55 + 10.65i$$

Division

Multiply the numerator and denominator by the complex conjugate of the denominator.

$$\frac{a + bi}{c + di} = \frac{(a + bi) \cdot (c - di)}{(c + di) \cdot (c - di)} = \frac{(a \cdot c + b \cdot d) + (-a \cdot d + b \cdot c)i}{c^2 + d^2}$$

Examples:

$$\frac{2 + 1.5i}{1 + 2i} = \frac{(2 + 1.5i) \cdot (1 - 2i)}{(1 + 2i) \cdot (1 - 2i)} = \frac{(2 + 3) + (-4 + 1.5)i}{1 + 4}$$

$$= \frac{5 - 2.5i}{5} = 1 - 0.5i$$

$$\frac{1}{4 + 2i} = \frac{1 \cdot (4 - 2i)}{(4 + 2i) \cdot (4 - 2i)} = \frac{4 - 2i}{16 + 4}$$

$$= \frac{4 - 2i}{20} = 0.2 - 0.1i$$

Name: _____ Date: _____

Lesson One: Exercises

Cardinal, ordinal, and nominal numbers.

1. State whether the following numbers are **cardinal**, **ordinal**, or **nominal** numbers.

   a) There are **five** players on a basketball team. _____

   b) Melissa was the **first** choice for class president. _____

   c) The policeman's badge number was **2012**. _____

   d) Norbert lives at **2134** Elm Street. _____

   e) **Third** place in a horse race is called "show." _____

   f) There are **100** years in a century. _____

Natural numbers, whole numbers, and integers.

2. State whether the following sets of numbers represent the **natural numbers**, the **whole numbers**, or the **integers**.

   a) {0, 1, 2, 3, 4,...} _____

   b) {1, 2, 3, 4, 5,...} _____

   c) {..., -3, -2, -1, 0, 1, 2, 3,...} _____

3. Write the elements in the following sets (enclose each set of elements in curly braces).

   a) The set of natural numbers less than 4. _____

   b) The set of natural numbers greater than 3, but less than 9. _____

   c) The set of whole numbers less than 5. _____

   d) The set of whole numbers between 4 and 10. _____

   e) The set of positive integers less than 4. _____

   f) The set of negative integers greater than -4. _____

Name: _____ Date: _____

Lesson One: Exercises (cont.)

4. Which of the following statements are true and which ones are false. Mark a "T" if the statement is true, or "F" if the statement is false on the blank provided.

   ___ **a)** The set {0, 1, 2, 3, 5, 7} is a subset of the natural numbers.

   ___ **b)** The set {0, 1, 2} is a subset of the whole numbers.

   ___ **c)** The set of natural numbers is closed with respect to subtraction.

   ___ **d)** The set of integers is commutative with respect to subtraction.

   ___ **e)** The set of whole numbers is closed with respect to addition.

Rational Numbers

5. Write the following rational numbers as fractions (in lowest terms) with integers in the numerators and integers in the denominators.

   a) 0.5 _____

   b) 0.125 _____

   c) 2.25 _____

   d) 1.666666... _____

   e) 1.8 _____

   f) 2.4 _____

   g) 1.1666666... _____

   h) 2.333333... _____

6. On your calculator, compute the following: $\frac{1}{9}, \frac{2}{9}, \frac{3}{9}, \frac{4}{9}, \frac{5}{9}, \frac{6}{9}, \frac{7}{9}, \frac{8}{9}.$

   Comment on your results. _____

   _____

   _____

   _____

   _____

Name: _____ Date: _____

Lesson One: Exercises (cont.)

Irrational Numbers

7. Use your calculator to compute the values of the following numbers. Are they all irrational?

a) $\sqrt{7}$ _____   **b)** $\sqrt{11}$ _____

c) $\sqrt{5}$ _____   **d)** $\sqrt{17}$ _____

e) $\sqrt{19}$ _____

Numbers

8. Which property of the real numbers is indicated by each of the following?

a) $2.0 + (0.5 + 3.0) = (2.0 + 0.5) + 3.0$ _____

b) $4.5(2.25 \cdot 2.0) = (4.5 \cdot 2.25)2.0$ _____

c) $0.0 \cdot 2.5 = 0.0$ _____

d) $2.0(3.0 + 4.0) = 2.0 \cdot 3.0 + 2.0 \cdot 4.0$ _____

e) $3.0 \left(\dfrac{1}{3.0}\right) = 1.0$ _____

f) $4.25 + 3.75 = 3.75 + 4.25$ _____

9. Show the following by a counter example:

a) The real numbers are not associative with respect to division.

_____

b) The real numbers are not commutative with respect to division.

_____

c) The real numbers are not commutative with respect to subtraction.

_____

Absolute Values

10. Find the absolute values of the following numbers.

a) $|\,12\,|$ _____   **b)** $|\,-167\,|$ _____   **c)** $|\,125.25\,|$ _____

d) $|\,-15.67\,|$ _____   **e)** $|\,-0.125\,|$ _____

Name: _____ Date: _____

Lesson One: Exercises (cont.)

Complete the following problems on your own paper.

Complex Numbers

11. Find the modulus of the following complex numbers. Plot the complex number on a graph and show the modulus.

    a) $4 - 3i$ **b)** $-12 + 5i$

    c) $2 + 3i$ **d)** $2.2 + 6.4i$

12. Find the complex conjugate of the following complex numbers. Plot the complex number and its complex conjugate on a graph.

    a) $4 - 3i$ **b)** $-12 + 5i$

    c) $2 + 3i$ **d)** $2.2 + 6.4i$

13. Find the sums of the following complex numbers.

    a) $(2 + 3i) + (1 + 2i)$ **b)** $(6 - 5i) + (4 - 3i)$

    c) $(8 - 2i) + (4 - 3i)$ **d)** $(2 + 3i) + (4 + 5i)$

    e) $(6 - 5i) + (-4 + 3i)$ **f)** $7 + (-9 - 7i)$

    g) $(-3 + 2i) + (1 + 5i)$ **h)** $(-5i) + (4 - 3i)$

    i) $(9.2 - 1.4i) + (4.4 - 3i)$

14. Perform the following complex subtractions.

    a) $(2 + 3i) - (1 + 2i)$ **b)** $(6 - 5i) - (4 - 3i)$

    c) $(8 - 2i) - (4 - 3i)$ **d)** $(2 + 3i) - (4 + 5i)$

    e) $(6 - 5i) - (-4 + 3i)$ **f)** $7 - (-9 - 7i)$

    g) $(-3 + 2i) - (1 + 5i)$ **h)** $(-5i) - (4 - 3i)$

    i) $(9.2 - 1.4i) - (4.4 - 3i)$

Name: _____ Date: _____

Lesson One: Exercises (cont.)

15. Perform the following complex multiplications.

    a) $(2 + 3i) \cdot (2 - 1i)$

    b) $(4 + 3i) \cdot (6 - 5i)$

    c) $(8 - 2i) \cdot (4 - 3i)$

    d) $(2 + 3i) \cdot (2 + 1i)$

    e) $(-4 + 3i) \cdot (6 - 5i)$

    f) $(-8 - 2i) \cdot (4 - 3i)$

    g) $5 \cdot (2 - 1i)$

    h) $7i \cdot (6 - 5i)$

    i) $(3.5 - 2.2i) \cdot (4.4 - 3.9i)$

16. Perform the following complex divisions. Simplify the resulting expressions so that there are no *i* items in the denominator.

    a) $\dfrac{2 - 3i}{1 + 1i}$

    b) $\dfrac{4 + 5i}{2 + 2i}$

    c) $\dfrac{8 - 2i}{4 - 3i}$

    d) $\dfrac{7 - 5i}{2 + 1i}$

    e) $\dfrac{5 + 3i}{2 - 2i}$

    f) $\dfrac{6 - 2i}{3 - 2i}$

    g) $\dfrac{12 - 6i}{3}$

    h) $\dfrac{48}{6 + 4i}$

    i) $\dfrac{4.4 - 2.3i}{1.8 - 3.6i}$

Lesson Two: Linear Functions and Equations

Juan was performing a science experiment with electrical voltages and currents. "Wow," he exclaimed, "the more voltage I apply, the more current I get. If I double the voltage, the current doubles, and if I triple the voltage, the current triples."

"You have just made an important discovery," his science teacher replied. "The current is linearly related to the voltage. The amount of current that flows in your circuit is proportional to the amount of voltage that you apply."

LINEAR RELATIONS

Like Juan, most of us have noticed things that appear to be related linearly. An increase or decrease in one quantity is proportional to an increase or decrease in another, related quantity. We can describe relations like these with linear equations and linear functions.

LINEAR EQUATIONS

You probably remember, from your algebra class, that equations are ways to state, mathematically, that two things are equal. A number or algebraic expression on the left-hand side of an equal sign is equal to another number or algebraic expression on the right-hand side of the equal sign.

A **linear equation** is a very special kind of equation, called a **first-degree equation**. A linear equation may contain any number of variables, but we will be interested in linear equations that contain only two variables. Each of these variables appears in the equation only once and only to the first power (only to a power of 1). There are no terms involving the product of the variables. The following examples are linear equations.

$$y = 5x + 7 \qquad\qquad a + 4 = b - 6$$

$$3z - 2 = 4y + 9 \qquad\qquad 2(q - 6) = 3(p + 5)$$

Lesson Two: Linear Functions and Equations (cont.)

THE GRAPH OF A LINEAR EQUATION

The graph of a linear equation is always a straight line. If one of the variables is plotted on the vertical axis of a rectangular coordinate system and the other one is plotted on the horizontal axis, the points will define a straight line. The straight lines below are graphs of the equations,

$y = 2x + 6$ and $y = 4x - 8$

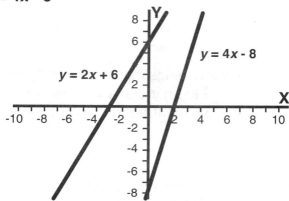

Since all of the points fall along the same straight line, it is only necessary to plot two points and then draw a straight line between them. All of the other points fall along the same line. Two points on the graph are sufficient to define a line.

LINEAR EQUATIONS FROM TWO POINTS

Since two points define a straight line, it is possible to get the equation of a line that passes through two points on a graph. If one of the points is **x1**, **y1**, and the other point is **x2**, **y2**, the equation of the straight line can be written as:

$$\frac{y - y1}{y2 - y1} = \frac{x - x1}{x2 - x1}$$

Example: Find the equation of the straight line through the points **x1 = 1**, **y1 = 1**, and **x2 = 2**, **y2 = 4**.

$$\frac{y - 1}{4 - 1} = \frac{x - 1}{2 - 1}$$

$$\frac{y - 1}{3} = \frac{x - 1}{1}$$

$$1(y - 1) = 3(x - 1)$$

$$y - 1 = 3x - 3$$

$$y = 3x - 2$$

Lesson Two: Linear Functions and Equations (cont.)

THE SLOPE OF A LINEAR EQUATION

A linear equation is often described by a quantity called its **slope** and a second quantity, either its **vertical intercept** or its **horizontal intercept**.

The **slope** of a line is determined by any two points on the line. It is defined as:

$$\text{slope} = m = \frac{\text{vertical change between the two points}}{\text{horizontal change between the two points}}$$

The vertical change between the two points is sometimes called the **rise**, and the horizontal change between the points is sometimes called the **run**. The slope is often denoted by the symbol **m**.

The graph below shows two straight lines and graphical views of their slopes.

$y = \frac{1}{2}x + 2$

$y = -2x$

The slope of a line can easily be computed by picking any two points, x_1, y_1 and x_2, y_2 on the line and using their values in the following equation.

$$\text{slope} = m = \frac{y_2 - y_1}{x_2 - x_1}$$

A slope is **positive** if the line slants upward to the right. It is **negative** if it slants downward to the right. The larger the magnitude of the slope, the more inclined the line. The slope of a horizontal line is **zero** and the slope of a vertical line is **infinitely large**.

Example: Find the slope of the straight line that passes through the points
$x_1 = -1$, $y_1 = 1$, and $x_2 = 2$, $y_2 = 7$.

$$m = \frac{7 - 1}{2 - (-1)} = \frac{6}{3}$$

$$= 2$$

Lesson Two: Linear Functions and Equations (cont.)

THE VERTICAL AND HORIZONTAL INTERCEPTS

The **vertical intercept** of a line is the point at which the line crosses the vertical axis of its graph. At this point, the value of the variable plotted on the horizontal axis is zero, and the value of the one plotted on the vertical axis is equal to the vertical intercept. (Because **y** is often the variable plotted on the vertical axis, the vertical intercept is sometimes called the **y-intercept**). The vertical intercept can easily be found from the graph of a linear equation. It can also be found from the equation by setting the horizontal variable to zero and solving the remaining portion of the equation for the vertical variable.

Example: Find the vertical intercept of the equation, $2y = -4x - 5$.

Setting $x = 0$, gives

$2y = -4 (0) - 5$

$y = -2.5$

The y-intercept is -2.5.

The **horizontal intercept** (sometimes called the **x-intercept**) is the point at which the line crosses the horizontal axis. At this point, the value of the vertical variable is zero.

Example: Find the horizontal intercept of the equation, $y - 2 = 3x + 1$

Setting $y = 0$, gives

$-2 = 3x + 1$

$3x = -3$

$x = -1$

The x-intercept is -1.

FORMS OF LINEAR EQUATIONS

The equation of a straight line can be written in several forms. Each of them can be converted to the others by performing a little algebra.

Slope-intercept form

$y = $ **slope** $x + $ **y-intercept,** or

$y = mx + b$ where m is the slope and b is the y-intercept.

Lesson Two: Linear Functions and Equations (cont.)

Point-slope form

$$y - y1 = m(x - x1)$$ where **m** is the slope and **x1, y1** is a point on the line

General linear equation form

$$Ax + By = C$$ where **A**, **B**, and **C** are numbers

Intercept form

$$\frac{x}{a} + \frac{y}{b} = 1$$ where **a** is the horizontal intercept and **b** is the vertical intercept

Example: Convert the linear equation, **y = -2x + 4**, to: (1) intercept form, and (2) general form.

Intercept form	**General form**
$y = -2x + 4$	$y = -2x + 4$
$2x + y = 4$	$2x + y = 4$
$\dfrac{2x}{2} + \dfrac{y}{4} = 1$	
$\dfrac{x}{1} + \dfrac{y}{4} = 1$	

PARALLEL AND PERPENDICULAR LINES

Two lines or linear equations are **parallel** if their slopes are equal. (If their intercepts are also equal, they are the same line).

Two lines or linear equations are **perpendicular** (the two lines intersect at right angles on a graph) if the product of their slopes is -1.

$$m1(m2) = -1$$

Example: Find the slope of a line that is perpendicular to the line, $y = -\dfrac{2}{5}x + 5$

The slope of this line is $-\frac{2}{5}$

$$-\tfrac{2}{5}(m2) = -1$$

$$m2 = \tfrac{5}{2}$$

Lesson Two: Linear Functions and Equations (cont.)

LINEAR FUNCTIONS

A **function** is a correspondence between two sets of values. One of these sets is called the **domain**, and the other one is called the **range**. Each value in the domain corresponds to precisely one value in the range. The function provides a rule for determining the value in the range that corresponds to a given value in the domain.

The equations that we have been looking at can be thought of as linear functions. The domain for these functions is the real numbers. The range is also the real numbers. The rule for determining the value in the range is usually indicated by the symbol f, followed by a variable in parentheses. For example, $f(x)$. The variable in parentheses represents a value from the domain.

The linear equations that we have looked at in this lesson can be written in function form as:

$$y = f(x) = mx + b$$

Some examples of linear functions are shown below:

$$f(x) = 6x - 4 \qquad\qquad f(x) = 8(x - 3)$$

$$f(p) = -3q + 11 \qquad\qquad f(u) = -5v + 1$$

A value in the range of the function can be obtained by giving the function a value from the domain and computing the value in the range. This is sometimes called **evaluating the function** at a certain value.

For example, look at the function $f(x) = 3x + 2$

For $x = 2$, $f(2) = 3(2) + 2 = 8$

For $x = 3$, $f(3) = 3(3) + 2 = 11$

For $x = -2$, $f(-2) = 3(-2) + 2 = -4$

Name: _____ Date: _____

Lesson Two: Exercises

Complete the following exercises on your own paper.

1. Graph the following linear equations on rectangular coordinate graph paper. Plot the **y** values on the vertical axis and the **x** values on the horizontal axis.

   a) $y = 3x - 2$ **b)** $y = -2x + 1$ **c)** $y = \frac{1}{2}x + 5$

2. Graph the line that passes through the indicated points on rectangular coordinate graph paper. Plot the **y** values on the vertical axis and the **x** values on the horizontal axis.

   a) (3, -2) (1, 3)   **b)** (-2, -1) (4, 5)   **c)** (0, 3) (4, 0)

3. Graph the line that has the indicated slope, **m**, and y-intercept, **b**.

   a) $m = 2, b = -3$ **b)** $m = -\frac{1}{2}, b = 5$ **c)** $m = -3, b = -1$

4. Write the equation of the line with slope, **m**, and vertical intercept, **b**.

   a) $m = 3, b = 4$ **b)** $m = -\frac{1}{4}, b = \frac{1}{2}$ **c)** $m = -4, b = -6$

   d) $m = \frac{1}{2}, b = -2$ **e)** $m = 1.25, b = -5.5$ **f)** $m = 0, b = 3$

5. Write the equation of the line passing through the given point with the given slope, **m**, in point-slope form. Simplify the equation to the slope-intercept form.

   a) (1, 1) $m = 2$ **b)** (-3, 2) $m = -3$ **c)** (2, 0.5) $m = -0.5$

   d) (-6, 3) $m = \frac{4}{3}$ **e)** (0, 0) $m = 8$ **f)** $(-\frac{3}{4}, \frac{3}{5})$ $m = 1$

6. Write the equation of the line through the given points. Simplify the equation to the slope-intercept form.

   a) (1, 1) (-1, -1)   **b)** (2, 0) (0, -2)   **c)** (4, 2) (2, 4)

   d) $(\frac{1}{2}, 2)$ $(-4, -\frac{3}{2})$ **e)** (1, 13) (8, -1)   **f)** (5, 2) (0, 0)

7. Find the slopes of the following linear equations.

   a) $3.5y + 7x = 4.4$ **b)** $5(y - 1) = -4(x + 2)$ **c)** $y = 9x - 6$

   d) $2y = x + 19$ **e)** $-3y + 6x = 0$ **f)** $x + y = 5$

Name: _____ Date: _____

Lesson Two: Exercises (cont.)

8. Find the vertical intercepts of the following linear equations.

    a) $2y + 7x = 4$ **b)** $5(y - 1) = 3(x + 2)$ **c)** $y = 17x - 6$

    d) $y = x + 19$ **e)** $-3y + 6x = 13$ **f)** $x + y = 18$

9. Find the horizontal intercepts of the following linear equations.

    a) $2y + 3x = 6$ **b)** $2(y - 1) = 3(x + 2)$ **c)** $y = 4x - 10$

    d) $y = x + 3$ **e)** $-3y + 6x = 13$ **f)** $x + y = 18$

10. Convert the following linear equations to slope-intercept form.

    a) $\dfrac{y}{4} + \dfrac{x}{2} = 1$ **b)** $2(y + 1) = 6(x + 2)$ **c)** $4y + 5x = 2$

11. Convert the following linear equations to intercept form.

    a) $4y = -2x + 4$ **b)** $y = \frac{2}{3}x + 6$ **c)** $y = -0.5x + 2$

12. Find the slopes of lines perpendicular to the ones below.

    a) $y = 0.5x + 2$ **b)** $y = -0.2x + 3$ **c)** $y = -2x + 1$

13. Which of the following pairs of lines are parallel?

    a) $y = 3x + 2$ **b)** $y = 5x + 5$ **c)** $2y = 4x + 1$
        $y = 5x + 2$ $y = 5x - 2$ $y = 2x - 10$

14. Evaluate the following linear functions at the domain values that are indicated.

    a) $f(x) = -6x + 3$ Find $f(2), f(5),$ and $f(-3)$

    b) $f(p) = 7p - 5$ Find $f(1), f(-5),$ and $f(6)$

    c) $f(v) = 0.5v + 1.5$ Find $f(2), f(-3),$ and $f(0.5)$

    d) $f(x) = 3(x + 2)$ Find $f(-4), f(0),$ and $f(3)$

    e) $f(x) = x + 1$ Find $f(-1.5), f(2.5),$ and $f(10)$

    f) $f(x) = 3.5x - 5.25$ Find $f(2), f(2.5),$ and $f(-1.5)$

Lesson Three: Linear Inequalities

Jason was playing a complicated computer game. "Yo," he said to his friend Mark, "I have a problem here. The character that I play in this game can have two kinds of special powers. The sum of the two powers must be less than or equal to 100. I've been trying to write this in some kind of equation, but it doesn't seem to work."

"That's your problem," replied Mark. "You can't write something like that as an equation, like $x + y = 100$, because it's not an equation. You need to write it as a linear inequality, $x + y \leq 100$."

INEQUALITIES

Some mathematical problems cannot be expressed as equations, where something on one side of an equal sign is equal to something on the other side. Instead, they are described by inequalities, where things are not necessarily equal. To explore inequalities, we will need some mathematical symbols other than the equal sign.

> **>**   This symbol stands for **greater than**. It says that something on its left-hand side is greater than something on its right-hand side.

> **<**   This symbol stands for **less than**. It says that something on its left-hand side is less than something on its right-hand side.

> **≥**   This symbol stands for **greater than or equal to**. It can be thought of as a combination of the greater than symbol and the equal sign.

> **≤**   This symbol stands for **less than or equal to**. It can be thought of as a combination of the less than symbol and the equal sign.

Some typical uses for these symbols and their meanings are shown below.

$x > 5$ x is greater than 5

$y < 10$ y is less than 10

$b \geq 25$ b is greater than or equal to 25

$z \leq -7$ z is less than or equal to -7

$3 < x < 7$ x is greater than 3 and less than 7

$-2 \leq y \leq 2$ y is greater than or equal to -2 and less than or equal to 2

$y + 2x < 5$ y plus 2 times x is less than 5

Lesson Three: Linear Inequalities (cont.)

These symbols can be used to describe **inequalities**. An inequality is different from an equation. An inequality states that two things are not equal, but not equal in a certain way. One type of inequality only involves one variable and is used to say that only a portion of the real numbers are of interest. For example, $x > 10.0$ says that x must be greater than 10. Graphically, this means that x must be on the portion of the real number line greater than 10.

Inequalities like the one above describe **intervals** on the real number line. An interval is the portion of the real number line where the inequality is satisfied. If the endpoint of an interval is defined by a > or < symbol, the interval is said to be an **open** interval. If the endpoint is defined by a ≥ or ≤ symbol, the interval is called **closed**.

If the interval extends to plus infinity or minus infinity, it is said to be **unbounded**. Otherwise, it is called **bounded**. The interval defined by $x > 10.0$ is an open, unbounded interval. It is open because of the > symbol, and it is unbounded because it extends to plus infinity.

It is interesting to show intervals as graphs on the real number line. A bold line is used to define the interval. An open circle is used to show an open endpoint of the interval, and a filled circle is used to show a closed endpoint. An arrow on one end of the line indicates an unbounded end of an interval. Some intervals and their graphs are shown below.

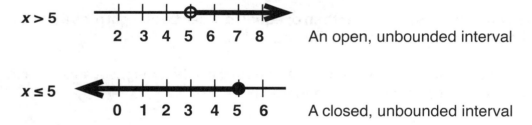

Bounded intervals must be defined by two inequalities, such as $x > 3$ and $x < 5$. The two inequalities can be combined into one expression, $3 < x < 5$. The following examples are bounded intervals.

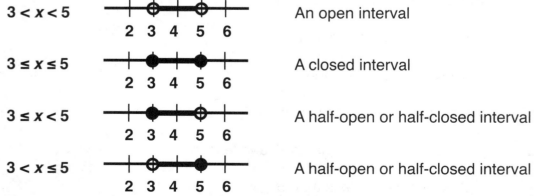

A doubly unbounded interval represents all of the real numbers.

Lesson Three: Linear Inequalities (cont.)

Open and closed intervals can also be represented by numbers in parentheses or brackets. Brackets are used to denote closed intervals and parentheses are used to indicate open intervals. The plus or minus infinity symbol is used to indicate unbounded intervals. Some examples are shown below.

(3, 5)	is the interval	$3 < x < 5$
[3, 5]	is the interval	$3 \leq x \leq 5$
[3, 5)	is the interval	$3 \leq x < 5$
(3, 5]	is the interval	$3 < x \leq 5$
[3, ∞)	is the interval	$x \geq 3$
(-∞, 3)	is the interval	$x < 3$

SOME REAL NUMBER PROPERTIES

Some interesting properties of real numbers can be expressed as inequalities.

Definition of $a < b$

For any two real numbers, **a** and **b**, $a < b$ if $b - a > 0$.

Similar definitions can be written for $a > b$, $a \leq b$, and $a \geq b$.

Trichotomy Property

For any two real numbers, **a** and **b**, only one of the following can be true: $a < b$, $a = b$, or $a > b$.

Addition Order Property

For any real numbers, **a**, **b**, and **c**, if $a < b$, then $a + c < b + c$.

Similar properties can be written for $a > b$, $a \leq b$, $a \geq b$.

Multiplication Order Property

For any real numbers, **a** and **b**, and **positive** real number **c**, if $a < b$, then $ac < bc$.

Similar properties can be written for $a > b$, $a \leq b$, $a \geq b$.

Lesson Three: Linear Inequalities (cont.)

For any real numbers, a and b, and **negative** real number c, if $a < b$, then $ac > bc$.

Similar properties can be written for $a > b$, $a \leq b$, $a \geq b$.

Transitive Order Property

For any real numbers a, b, and c, if $a < b$ and $b < c$, then $a < c$.

Similar properties can be written for $a > b$ and $b > c$, etc.

Addition Property

For any real numbers a, b, c, and d, if $a < b$ and $c < d$, then $a + c < b + d$.

Similar properties could be written for $a > b$ and $c > d$, etc.

Multiplication Property

For a, b, c, and d, all positive real numbers, if $a < b$ and $c < d$, then $ac < bd$.

Similar properties could be written for $a > b$ and $c > d$, etc.

Reciprocal Property

For real numbers a and b, if $a < b$ and $ab > 0$, then $\dfrac{1}{a} > \dfrac{1}{b}$

if $a > b$ and $ab > 0$, then $\dfrac{1}{a} < \dfrac{1}{b}$

Lesson Three: Linear Inequalities (cont.)

LINEAR INEQUALITIES

You have seen linear equations that involve two variables, each to the first power. If the equal sign in a linear equation is replaced by a $>$, $<$, $\geq$, or $\leq$ symbol, the equation becomes a linear inequality. Some linear inequalities are shown below:

$$y + 2x < 5 \qquad 3y - 4x \geq 6 \qquad x + y \leq 3 \qquad x - 3y > -2$$

Linear inequalities can be plotted on rectangular coordinate graphs. Their graphs, however, are not lines, but **half-planes**. As an example, consider the graph of $y + 2x \leq 5$.

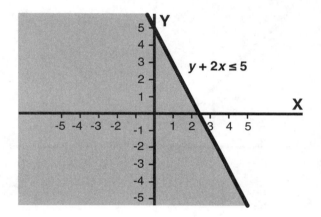

The graph can be constructed by first drawing the line $y + 2x = 5$ and then noting that this line divides the x-y plane into two half-planes. The half-plane that contains the x and y values that give $y + 2x \leq 5$ is shown shaded.

Graphs of $x + y \leq 3$ and $x + 3y > -2$ are shown below. A solid line is used to divide the x-y plane if a $\leq$ or $\geq$ symbol is present in the inequality. A dashed line is used if a $<$ or $>$ symbol is present.

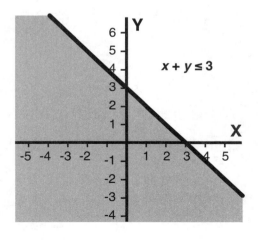

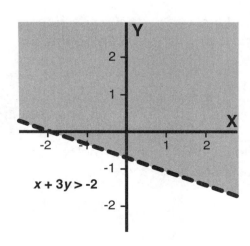

Lesson Three: Linear Inequalities (cont.)

GRAPHING ABSOLUTE VALUE FUNCTIONS

Inequalities can be used to help specify the graph of an **absolute value function**. Consider the following function.

$$y = f(x) = |x|$$

For positive **x** values, the graph of the function would be the line **y = x**. For negative values of **x**, however, the graph would be the line **y = -x**. The two lines would intersect at the origin.

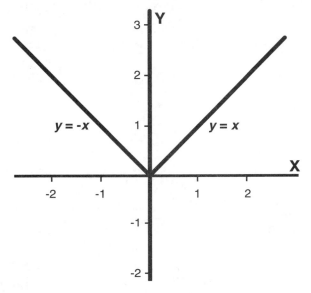

The absolute value function can be written in a form suggested by the graph.

$$y = f(x) = |x| = \begin{cases} x & \text{if } x \geq 0 \\ -x & \text{if } x < 0 \end{cases}$$

Other functions involving absolute values can be written in similar ways. For example, the function, $y = f(x) = |x - 4|$, can be written:

$$y = f(x) = |x - 4| = \begin{cases} x - 4 & \text{if } x \geq 4 \\ -x - 4 & \text{if } x < 4 \end{cases}$$

Its graph would look much like the one for $y = |x|$, except that the intersection of the two lines would occur at **x = 4** instead of 0.

Lesson Three: Linear Inequalities (cont.)

A very special function is called the **step function**. It can be written as:

$$y = f(x) = \frac{|x|}{x}$$

This function evaluates to 1 for $x \geq 0$, and to -1 for $x < 0$. Its graph and another way of writing the function are shown below.

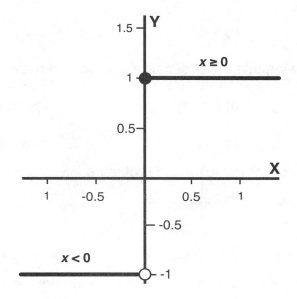

$$y = f(x) = \begin{cases} 1 & \text{if } x \geq 0 \\ -1 & \text{if } x < 0 \end{cases}$$

Name: _____   Date: _____

Lesson Three: Exercises

Complete the following exercises on your own paper.

1. Show the intervals below on the real number line. Use the appropriate symbols to show open, closed, bounded and unbounded intervals.

    a) $-5 \leq x \leq 2$ **b)** $-1 \leq x < 5$ **c)** $3 < x \leq 7$

    d) $-6 \leq x \leq -2$ **e)** $2 < x < 5$ **f)** $6 < x < 9$

    g) $x \geq 2$ **h)** $x < 5$ **i)** $x > 8$

2. Write each of the following intervals using the ≤, ≥, <, and > symbols.

    a) $(-\infty, -2]$ **b)** $(-1, \infty)$ **c)** $(-2, 5]$

    d) $[4, 8]$ **e)** $(-1, 1)$ **f)** $[6, 9)$

3. Select the correct answer for the following problems.

    a) For any real numbers, *a*, *b*, and *c*

        If $a \geq b$, then

        x) $a + c < b + c$ **y)** $a + c \geq b + c$ **z)** $a + c \leq b + c$

    b) For any real numbers, *a* and *b*, and <u>positive</u> real number *c*

        If $a > b$, then

        x) $ac < bc$ **y)** $ac \leq bc$ **z)** $ac > bc$

    c) For any real numbers, *a* and *b*, and <u>negative</u> real number *c*

        If $a > b$, then

        x) $ac < bc$ **y)** $ac \leq bc$ **z)** $ac > bc$

    d) For any real numbers *a*, *b*, and *c*

        If $a > b$ and $b > c$, then

        x) $a > c$ **y)** $a \leq c$ **z)** $a < c$

    e) For any real numbers, *a*, *b*, *c*, and *d*

        If $a > b$ and $c > d$, then

        x) $a + c < b + d$ **y)** $a + c > b + d$ **z)** $a + c = b + d$

Name: _____ Date: _____

Lesson Three: Exercises (cont.)

f) For a, b, c, and d, all positive real numbers

If $a < b$ and $c < d$, then

x) $ac \geq bd$ **y)** $ac > bd$ **z)** $ac < bd$

g) For real numbers a and b

If $a < b$ and $ab > 0$, then

x) $\frac{1}{a} > \frac{1}{b}$ **y)** $\frac{1}{a} \leq \frac{1}{b}$ **z)** $\frac{1}{a} < \frac{1}{b}$

4. Graph the following inequalities. Indicate the half-plane in which the inequality is satisfied.

a) $3x + 2y \leq 7$ **b)** $2y - x \geq 3$ **c)** $y < 2x + 5$

d) $y + x > 1$ **e)** $y \geq 2$ **f)** $x < 4$

5. Find the interval for x that satisfies the following inequalities.

Example: **$-2x + 1 > 5$**

$-2x + 1 - 1 > 5 - 1$

$-2x > 4$

$\frac{-2x}{-2} > \frac{4}{-2}$

$x < -2$

a) $2x - 4 \geq 6$ **b)** $x + 17 \leq 21$ **c)** $x + 1 < -1$

d) $2(x - 1) \geq 3$ **e)** $-3x + 5 \leq 10$ **f)** $-5x + 1 < -11$

g) $-9x \geq 36$ **h)** $7x \leq 21$ **i)** $-3(x + 1) < 27$

6. Graph the following absolute value functions.

a) $y = |x + 1|$ **b)** $y = |x - 3|$ **c)** $y = |2x - 1|$

d) $y = |5 - 2x|$ **e)** $y = |\frac{1}{2}x + 1|$ **f)** $y = |3x|$

Lesson Four: Quadratic Functions

Suzanne was watching intently as her next door neighbor, Jenny, was using a strange device to listen to distant bird calls. It was a large, dish-shaped piece of plastic with a microphone at its center. When Suzanne asked what it was, Jenny told her it was a parabolic microphone. It picked up sound from its entire surface and reflected it all to the microphone at the center. The parabolic shape of the plastic allowed the sound to be focused at the spot where the microphone was attached.

"How did you learn so much about parabolas?" Suzanne asked.

"From my pre-calculus math class," Jenny replied. "We studied quadratic equations, and a parabola is a quadratic equation."

QUADRATIC FUNCTIONS AND EQUATIONS

The last two lessons have talked about linear equations and linear inequalities. Sometimes, however, we need to look at equations and functions that are not linear. One group of **non-linear** functions and equations is called **quadratics**.

A **quadratic function** contains a term involving a variable to the second (square) power. It may also contain a term involving the first power of the variable, and/or a constant term. Some examples of quadratic functions are shown below.

$$f(x) = 3x^2 - 2x + 6$$

$$f(q) = 8q^2 + 19q$$

$$f(z) = 3z^2 + 10$$

$$f(x) = x^2$$

An equation in the form, $y = f(x)$, where $f(x)$ is a quadratic function, is called a **quadratic equation**.

$$y = 7x^2 + 5x$$

$$y = x^2 - x + 2$$

$$y = 2x^2 - 11$$

Quadratic equations have some special properties that are most easily seen on graphs. A graph of a quadratic equation can be produced from a table of values. Consider the equation, $y = x^2$. This is the simplest quadratic equation. When x is 1, y is 1; when x is 2, y is 4; when x is 3, y is 9, etc. Also, when x is -1, y is 1; when x is -2, y is 4; when x is -3, y is 9, etc. A more complete table and graph are shown on the next page.

Lesson Four: Quadratic Functions (cont.)

x	y
-5	25
-4	16
-3	9
-2	4
-1	1
0	0
1	1
2	4
3	9
4	16
5	25

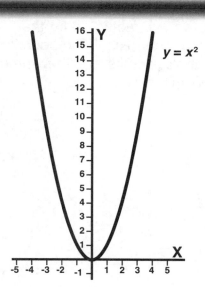

The graph of a quadratic equation, like the one above, is called a **parabola**. (The equation that is used to generate the graph is also called a parabola.) It is symmetric with respect to the vertical axis. Being **symmetric** means that it is the same on one side of the y-axis as it is on the other side. The turning point in the parabola is called the **vertex**. The vertex is the "tip" of the parabola. In the graph above, for $y = x^2$, the vertex is at the origin and the rest of the parabola extends upward. In a graph of $y = -x^2$, the vertex would still be at the origin, but the parabola would extend downward.

The parabola curve behaves differently on the two different sides of the vertex. In the graph above, the value of y decreases as x increases toward the vertex from the left. The function in this region is said to be **decreasing**. To the right of the vertex, the value of y increases as x increases away from the vertex. The function in this region is said to be **increasing**.

A parabola does not have to have its vertex at the origin, as the $y = x^2$ equation does. If the equation contains a constant term, then the parabola can have a vertex above or below the origin. The graphs below show plots of $y = x^2 + 4$ and $y = x^2 - 3$.

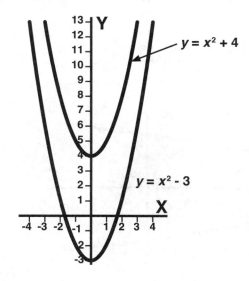

Lesson Four: Quadratic Functions (cont.)

Parabolas do not have to be symmetric about the *y*-axis. They can also be symmetric around some axis that is parallel to the *y*-axis. If the equation contains a term involving *x* to the first power, the vertex of the parabola, and its axis of symmetry, will be to the left or the right of the *y*-axis. Two examples are shown below.

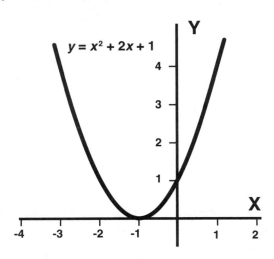

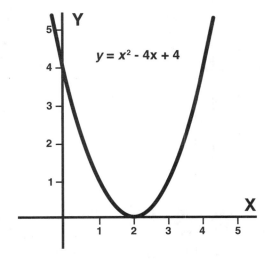

Parabolas can have vertices that are to the left or to the right of the *y*-axis and are also above or below the *x*-axis. They can open downward instead of upward. It is also possible to have a horizontal parabola if *x* is written as a function of *y*.

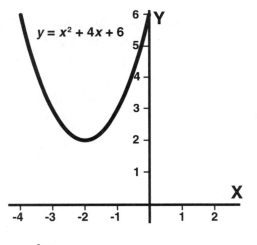

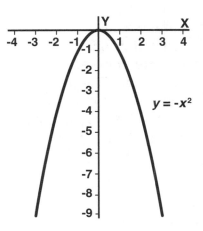

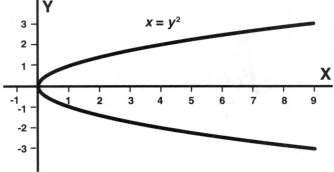

Lesson Four: Quadratic Functions (cont.)

SOLUTIONS TO QUADRATIC EQUATIONS

The most general form of a quadratic equation is $y = ax^2 + bx + c$, where a, b, and c are real numbers, and x and y are variables. Positions on the graph of such an equation where the plot crosses the x-axis are called the **x-intercepts**, or the **roots** of the equation. As can be seen in the graphs below, a quadratic equation can have two, one, or zero x-intercepts.

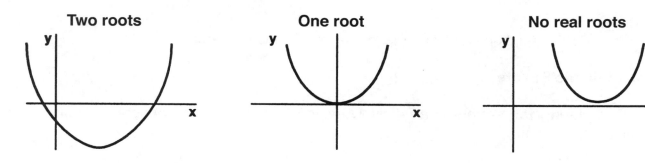

Two roots   **One root**   **No real roots**

The roots of a quadratic equation, $y = ax^2 + bx + c$, can be found by solving the equation, $ax^2 + bx + c = 0$. There are three ways to find a solution: (1) factor the equation; (2) complete the square, and (3) use the quadratic formula.

Factoring

In some cases, the equation can be easily factored. Then, each of the two factors can be set to zero and solved for an x-intercept value.

Examples:

1) $y = x^2$

$x^2 = 0$

$x(x) = 0 \qquad x = 0, \; x = 0$

$y = x^2$ has a double root at $x = 0$. It has only one x-intercept value.

2) $y = 2x^2 - 3x$

$2x^2 - 3x = 0$

$x(2x - 3) = 0 \qquad x = 0, \qquad 2x - 3 = 0$

$\qquad\qquad\qquad\qquad x = 0, \qquad x = \frac{3}{2}$

This equation has two roots, one at $x = 0$, and one at $x = \frac{3}{2}$.

Lesson Four: Quadratic Functions (cont.)

3) $y = x^2 - x - 6$

$x^2 - x - 6 = 0$

$(x - 3)(x + 2) = 0$ $x - 3 = 0,$ $x + 2 = 0$

                                $x = 3,$ $x = -2$

This equation has two roots, one at $x = 3$, and one at $x = -2$

Completing the Square

Completing the square is a relatively easy method for solving quadratic equations. It consists of three steps:

1. Write the square term and the first-power term on the left-hand side of the equation and transfer the constant term (if any) to the right-hand side. Then, divide through by the coefficient of the square term.

2. Add a real number to the left-hand side that makes that side a perfect square. Add the same number to the right-hand side.

3. Take the square root of both sides of the equation. Place a + or - in front of the value that you get on the right-hand side. Then solve by setting the left-hand side equal to + the right-hand side, and again by setting the left-hand side equal to - the right-hand side.

Examples:

1) $y = x^2 + x - 12$

$x^2 + x - 12 = 0$

$x^2 + x = 12$

$x^2 + x + \frac{1}{4} = 12 + \frac{1}{4} = \frac{49}{4}$

$(x + \frac{1}{2})^2 = \frac{49}{4}$

$(x + \frac{1}{2}) = \pm\frac{7}{2}$ $x + \frac{1}{2} = \frac{7}{2},$ $x + \frac{1}{2} = -\frac{7}{2}$

                                $x = \frac{7}{2} - \frac{1}{2} = 3$ $x = -\frac{7}{2} - \frac{1}{2} = -4$

Lesson Four: Quadratic Functions (cont.)

2) $y = 2x^2 - 3x - 2$

$2x^2 - 3x - 2 = 0$

$2x^2 - 3x = 2$

$x^2 - 3x/2 = 1$

$x^2 - 3x/2 + \frac{9}{16} = 1 + \frac{9}{16} = \frac{25}{16}$

$(x - \frac{3}{4})^2 = \pm\frac{5}{4}$ 　　　　$x - \frac{3}{4} = \frac{5}{4},$ 　　　　$x - \frac{3}{4} = -\frac{5}{4}$

　　　　　　　　　　$x = \frac{5}{4} + \frac{3}{4} = 2$ 　　　$x = -\frac{5}{4} + \frac{3}{4} = -\frac{1}{2}$

Quadratic Formula

Quadratic equations that are difficult to solve by factoring or completing the square can be solved with the **quadratic formula**. This formula can be derived by solving the general quadratic form, $ax^2 + bx + c = 0$, by completing the square. The roots of the equation can be expressed in terms of a, b, and c as follows:

$$x = \frac{-b}{2a} \pm \frac{\sqrt{b^2 - 4ac}}{2a}$$

The expression, $b^2 - 4ac$, inside the square root sign is called the **discriminant**. It determines whether there will be two roots, one (double) root, or no real roots to the equation. If there are no real roots, the quadratic formula can be used to find the complex roots of the equation. The three cases are described below.

1. $b^2 - 4ac > 0$　　　　The quadratic equation has two roots. Its graph crosses the x-axis twice.

2. $b^2 - 4ac = 0$　　　　The quadratic equation has only one root (a double root). The vertex of its graph touches the x-axis at only one point.

3. $b^2 - 4ac < 0$　　　　The quadratic equation has no real roots. Its graph does not intersect the x-axis. The equation does, however, have two roots that can be expressed as complex numbers.

Lesson Four: Quadratic Functions (cont.)

Examples:

1) $y = 2x^2 - 5x - 3$

$2x^2 - 5x - 3 = 0$

$$x = \frac{-(-5)}{2(2)} \pm \frac{\sqrt{-5^2 - 4(2)(-3)}}{2(2)}$$

$$= \frac{5}{4} \pm \frac{\sqrt{49}}{4} = \frac{5}{4} \pm \frac{7}{4}$$

$$x = \frac{5}{4} + \frac{7}{4} = 3$$

$$x = \frac{5}{4} - \frac{7}{4} = -\frac{1}{2}$$

2) $y = x^2 + 4x + 4$

$x^2 + 4x + 4 = 0$

$$x = \frac{-4}{2(1)} \pm \frac{\sqrt{4^2 - 4(1)(4)}}{2(1)}$$

$= -2$ **(double root)**

3) $y = x^2 - 2x + 5$

$x^2 - 2x + 5 = 0$

$$x = \frac{-(-2)}{2(1)} \pm \frac{\sqrt{-2^2 - 4(1)5}}{2(1)}$$

$$= 1 \pm \frac{\sqrt{-16}}{2} = 1 \pm \frac{4i}{2}$$

$$= 1 \pm 2i$$

$x = 1 + 2i$ $x = 1 - 2i$

Name: _____ Date: _____

Lesson Four: Exercises

Complete the following exercises on your own paper.

1. Sketch the graphs of the following quadratic equations.

    a) $y = x^2 - 5$ **b)** $y = -2x^2 + 1$

    c) $y = -3x^2$ **d)** $y = x^2 + 4x + 3$

    e) $y = x^2 + 4x + 4$ **f)** $y = 2x^2 - 5x - 12$

2. Find the real roots of the following quadratic equations by factoring.

    a) $y = x^2 + 2x + 1$ **b)** $y = x^2 - 6x + 8$

    c) $y = 4x^2 - 1$ **d)** $y = 4x^2 + 4x - 3$

    e) $y = x^2 + 4x + 3$ **f)** $y = x^2 - 10x + 25$

    g) $y = x^2 - 6x$ **h)** $y = 5x^2 + 4x$

    i) $y = 4x^2$

3. Find the real roots of the following quadratic equations by completing the square.

    a) $y = x^2 + 6x - 7$ **b)** $y = x^2 + 4x + 3$

    c) $y = 6x^2 - 5x + 1$ **d)** $y = x^2 + \frac{1}{2}x - \frac{1}{2}$

    e) $y = -2x^2 + 10x + 12$ **f)** $y = x^2 - 4x + 1$

4. Use the quadratic formula to find the real or complex roots of the following quadratic equations. Use your calculator to find square roots.

    a) $y = x^2 + 7x + 12$ **b)** $y = 6x^2 + x - 1$

    c) $y = x^2 - 10x + 25$ **d)** $y = x^2 + x - 3$

    e) $y = x^2 - 2x + 5$ **f)** $y = 2x^2 + 2x + 1$

Lesson Five: Polynomials and Rational Expressions

Janet was convinced that her older brother had a new girlfriend. He was on the phone with his best friend, and she kept hearing the word *Polly.*

"Who is Polly?" she said, smugly, after he had hung up.

"Polly is not a who," he answered. "It is a math function called a polynomial. We are studying polynomials in my pre-calculus class."

"When will I learn about polynomials?" Janet asked.

"In a few more years," her brother replied. "About the same time you learn not to eavesdrop on telephone conversations."

POLYNOMIALS

Linear and quadratic functions and equations are not the only expressions of interest in mathematics. Polynomials are also important. A **polynomial** is an algebraic expression involving two or more terms. A **term** in a polynomial can be a number, a variable to a positive integer power, or a product of numbers and variables to positive integer powers. Some polynomials are shown below.

$$y = 2x^3 - 3x^2 - 6x + 3$$

$$y = 12x^3 - 19x$$

$$y = \tfrac{1}{2}x^3 - 3x^2 - 6x + 3$$

$$y = -3x^4 + \tfrac{1}{4}x^2 + 3x$$

$$y = 4x^5 + 7x^4 - 9x^3 + 2x^2 - 11x + 13$$

The **degree** of a polynomial is the largest power of the variable in the polynomial. In the examples above, the first equation is of degree 3 (because of the x^3 term), and the last equation is of degree 5 (because of the x^5 term). The numbers that are next to the variables in the terms are called **coefficients**. The first equation has coefficients 2, -3, -6, and 3, and the last equation has coefficients 4, 7, -9, 2, -11, and 13.

A polynomial that has only one term (for example, $y = 5x^4$) is called a **monomial**. One that has only two terms (for example, $y = 2x^3 - x$) is called a **binomial**. One that has three terms (for example, $y = x^2 - 3x + 2$) is known as a **trinomial**. Others are simply called polynomials.

Note: It is possible to have polynomials in more than one variable. We will only be interested in polynomials in one variable.

Lesson Five: Polynomials and Rational Expressions (cont.)

Polynomials are usually written in **standard form**. Standard form involves writing the terms in order of ascending powers of the variable or in order of descending powers of the variable. The polynomials in the example on the previous page are all written in standard form, with the powers of **x** in descending order. A term that contains only a number is sometimes called the **constant term**. It is important to realize, however, that it is really a real number times x^0. You should remember that x^0 is 1.

ADDING AND SUBTRACTING POLYNOMIALS

Adding and subtracting polynomials is easy. You only need to remember to add or subtract coefficients of like powers of the variable. The addition or subtraction is easier if you arrange each of the polynomials in standard form. The following examples show how polynomials can be added and subtracted.

Example: Add $2x^3 - 5x^2 + 3$ to $2x^3 + 7x^2 + 3x + 2$

$$\begin{array}{r} 2x^3 - 5x^2 \quad\quad + 3 \\ + 2x^3 + 7x^2 + 3x + 2 \\ \hline 4x^3 + 2x^2 + 3x + 5 \end{array}$$

Example: Subtract $x^3 - 2x^2 + 3x + 2$ from $3x^3 + 3x^2 + 5x + 9$

$$\begin{array}{r} 3x^3 + 3x^2 + 5x + 9 \\ - (x^3 - 2x^2 + 3x + 2) \\ \hline 2x^3 + 5x^2 + 2x + 7 \end{array}$$

MULTIPLYING POLYNOMIALS

Polynomials are multiplied term by term, using the distributive property. It is sometimes easier to write one polynomial below the other one and multiply them like you would multi-digit numbers using partial products. The following examples show two ways to multiply polynomials.

Example: Multiply $x^2 - 3x + 1$ by $2x^2 + 2x + 4$

In this example, each term in the first polynomial is multiplied by each term in the second one.

$$(x^2 - 3x + 1)(2x^2 + 2x + 4) = (x^2)(2x^2) + (x^2)(2x) + (x^2)4 + (-3x)(2x^2) +$$

$$(-3x)(2x) + (-3x)4 + 1(2x^2) + 1(2x) + 1(4)$$

$$= 2x^4 + 2x^3 + 4x^2 - 6x^3 - 6x^2 - 12x + 2x^2 + 2x + 4$$

$$= 2x^4 - 4x^3 - 10x + 4$$

Lesson Five: Polynomials and Rational Expressions (cont.)

Example: Multiply $x^2 - 3x + 1$ by $2x^2 + 2x + 4$

In this example, the polynomials are written one above the other and multiplied like multi-digit numbers. The partial products are added to give the final product.

$$
\begin{array}{r}
x^2 - 3x + 1 \\
2x^2 + 2x + 4 \\
\hline
4x^2 - 12x + 4 \\
2x^3 - 6x^2 + 2x \\
2x^4 - 6x^3 + 2x^2 \\
\hline
2x^4 - 4x^3 + 0x^2 - 10x + 4
\end{array}
$$

Answer: $2x^4 - 4x^3 - 10x + 4$

DIVIDING POLYNOMIALS

Polynomials can be divided in a way that is a little like ordinary long division of numbers. To see how polynomial division is performed, consider the step-by-step example below.

Example: Divide $3x^3 + 8x^2 + x - 2$ by $x^2 + 2x - 1$

1) Write the division operation as shown below.

$$x^2 + 2x - 1 \,\overline{\big)\, 3x^3 + 8x^2 + x - 2}$$

2) The first term of the quotient is the first term of the divisor divided into the first term of the dividend.

$$
\begin{array}{r}
3x \\
x^2 + 2x - 1 \,\overline{\big)\, 3x^3 + 8x^2 + x - 2}
\end{array}
$$

3) Multiply the divisor by the quotient term and subtract from the first three terms of the dividend.

$$
\begin{array}{r}
3x \\
x^2 + 2x - 1 \,\overline{\big)\, 3x^3 + 8x^2 + x - 2} \\
\underline{3x^3 + 6x^2 - 3x} \\
2x^2 + 4x
\end{array}
$$

4) Bring down the next term to the right in the dividend.

$$
\begin{array}{r}
3x \\
x^2 + 2x - 1 \,\overline{\big)\, 3x^3 + 8x^2 + x - 2} \\
\underline{3x^3 + 6x^2 - 3x} \cdot \\
2x^2 + 4x - 2
\end{array}
$$

Lesson Five: Polynomials and Rational Expressions (cont.)

5) The second term in the quotient is found as in step 2. Divide the first term of the divisor into the first term of the $2x^2 + 4x - 2$.

$$x^2 + 2x - 1 \overline{\smash{\big)}\begin{array}{r} 3x + 2 \\ 3x^3 + 8x^2 + x - 2 \\ \underline{3x^3 + 6x^2 - 3x} \\ 2x^2 + 4x - 2 \end{array}}$$

6) Multiply the divisor by the right-hand quotient term and subtract from the $2x^2 + 4x - 2$.

$$x^2 + 2x - 1 \overline{\smash{\big)}\begin{array}{r} 3x + 2 \\ 3x^3 + 8x^2 + x - 2 \\ \underline{3x^3 + 6x^2 - 3x} \\ 2x^2 + 4x - 2 \\ \underline{2x^2 + 4x - 2} \\ 0 \end{array}}$$

The subtraction leaves a 0, and there are no more quotient terms to bring down, so the division operation is complete. The quotient is $3x + 2$.

Example: As a second example, consider $2x^4 - 3x^3 - 5x^2 + 7x - 2$ divided by $x - 2$.

$$x - 2 \overline{\smash{\big)} 2x^4 - 3x^3 - 5x^2 + 7x - 2}$$

$$x - 2 \overline{\smash{\big)}\begin{array}{r} 2x^3 \\ 2x^4 - 3x^3 - 5x^2 + 7x - 2 \\ \underline{2x^4 - 4x^3} \\ x^3 \end{array}}$$

$$x - 2 \overline{\smash{\big)}\begin{array}{r} 2x^3 \\ 2x^4 - 3x^3 - 5x^2 + 7x - 2 \\ \underline{2x^4 - 4x^3} \quad \cdot \\ x^3 - 5x^2 \end{array}}$$

$$x - 2 \overline{\smash{\big)}\begin{array}{r} 2x^3 + x^2 \\ 2x^4 - 3x^3 - 5x^2 + 7x - 2 \\ \underline{2x^4 - 4x^3} \\ x^3 - 5x^2 \\ \underline{x^3 - 2x^2} \\ - 3x^2 \end{array}}$$

Lesson Five: Polynomials and Rational Expressions (cont.)

$$
\begin{array}{r}
2x^3 + x^2 \phantom{{}- 5x^2 + 7x - 2} \\
x - 2 \overline{)\; 2x^4 - 3x^3 - 5x^2 + 7x - 2} \\
\underline{2x^4 - 4x^3} \phantom{{}- 5x^2 + 7x - 2} \quad \bullet \\
x^3 - 5x^2 \phantom{{}+ 7x - 2} \quad \bullet \\
\underline{x^3 - 2x^2} \phantom{{}+ 7x - 2} \quad \bullet \\
- 3x^2 + 7x \phantom{{}- 2}
\end{array}
$$

$$
\begin{array}{r}
2x^3 + x^2 - 3x \phantom{{}+ 7x - 2} \\
x - 2 \overline{)\; 2x^4 - 3x^3 - 5x^2 + 7x - 2} \\
\underline{2x^4 - 4x^3} \phantom{{}- 5x^2 + 7x - 2} \\
x^3 - 5x^2 \phantom{{}+ 7x - 2} \\
\underline{x^3 - 2x^2} \phantom{{}+ 7x - 2} \\
- 3x^2 + 7x \phantom{{}- 2} \\
\underline{- 3x^2 + 6x} \phantom{{}- 2} \\
x \phantom{{}- 2}
\end{array}
$$

$$
\begin{array}{r}
2x^3 + x^2 - 3x \phantom{{}+ 7x - 2} \\
x - 2 \overline{)\; 2x^4 - 3x^3 - 5x^2 + 7x - 2} \\
\underline{2x^4 - 4x^3} \phantom{{}- 5x^2 + 7x - 2} \quad \bullet \\
x^3 - 5x^2 \phantom{{}+ 7x - 2} \quad \bullet \\
\underline{x^3 - 2x^2} \phantom{{}+ 7x - 2} \quad \bullet \\
- 3x^2 + 7x \phantom{{}- 2} \quad \bullet \\
\underline{- 3x^2 + 6x} \phantom{{}- 2} \quad \bullet \\
x - 2
\end{array}
$$

$$
\begin{array}{r}
2x^3 + x^2 - 3x + 1 \phantom{{}7x - 2} \\
x - 2 \overline{)\; 2x^4 - 3x^3 - 5x^2 + 7x - 2} \\
\underline{2x^4 - 4x^3} \phantom{{}- 5x^2 + 7x - 2} \\
x^3 - 5x^2 \phantom{{}+ 7x - 2} \\
\underline{x^3 - 2x^2} \phantom{{}+ 7x - 2} \\
- 3x^2 + 7x \phantom{{}- 2} \\
\underline{- 3x^2 + 6x} \phantom{{}- 2} \\
x - 2 \\
\underline{x - 2} \\
0
\end{array}
$$

The quotient in this problem is $2x^3 + x^2 - 3x + 1$.

Lesson Five: Polynomials and Rational Expressions (cont.)

If the last subtraction in a division operation does not leave a zero, then there will be a remainder in the division problem. The remainder is the term left after the last subtraction. The example below shows a polynomial division that leaves a remainder.

Example: Divide $2x^3 - x^2 - 6x + 8$ by $x^2 + x - 2$

$$x^2 + x - 2 \enclose{longdiv}{2x^3 - x^2 - 6x + 8}$$

$$
\begin{array}{r}
2x \\
x^2 + x - 2 \enclose{longdiv}{2x^3 - x^2 - 6x + 8} \\
\underline{2x^3 + 2x^2 - 4x } \\
-3x^2 - 2x
\end{array}
$$

$$
\begin{array}{r}
2x \\
x^2 + x - 2 \enclose{longdiv}{2x^3 - x^2 - 6x + 8} \\
\underline{2x^3 + 2x^2 - 4x } \\
-3x^2 - 2x + 8
\end{array}
$$

$$
\begin{array}{r}
2x - 3 \\
x^2 + x - 2 \enclose{longdiv}{2x^3 - x^2 - 6x + 8} \\
\underline{2x^3 + 2x^2 - 4x } \\
-3x^2 - 2x + 8 \\
\underline{-3x^2 - 3x + 6 } \\
x + 2
\end{array}
$$

The quotient is $2x - 3$, and the remainder is $x + 2$.

Sometimes the divisor will simply be a variable to an integer power or a number times a variable to an integer power. In this case, the quotient can be found by dividing the divisor into each term of the dividend. You need to remember that a variable to a power divided by the same variable to another power is equal to that variable to the difference of the two powers.

$$\frac{x^a}{x^b} = x^{a-b}$$

The example below shows a polynomial divided by a variable to a power.

Example: Divide $2x^4 - 6x^3 + x^2$ by x^2

$$\frac{2x^4 - 6x^3 + x^2}{x^2} = \frac{2x^4}{x^2} - \frac{6x^3}{x^2} + \frac{x^2}{x^2}$$

$$= 2x^2 - 6x + 1$$

Lesson Five: Polynomials and Rational Expressions (cont.)

FACTORING POLYNOMIALS

It is often necessary to break a polynomial into two or more factors (if possible). **Factoring** can be thought of as the opposite process of multiplying polynomials. Sometimes polynomials can be factored by **inspection**, just by looking at the polynomial and noticing that it is the obvious product of certain terms. The examples below show some simple polynomials that can be factored by inspection.

$$x^2 + 3x + 2 = (x + 1)(x + 2)$$

$$x^2 - 5x + 6 = (x - 2)(x - 3)$$

$$x^3 - 2x^2 + x = x(x - 1)(x - 1)$$

Some forms, such as the trinomial that results from the square of a linear term, are easy to recognize.

$$(ax + b)^2 = a^2x^2 + 2abx + b^2$$

Example: Factor $4x^2 + 12x + 9$

$$4x^2 + 12x + 9 = (2x + 3)(2x + 3)$$

In other cases, there are special forms that can be used to identify factors. The simplest of these forms is the one involving the difference of two squares. Others involve the difference or sum of two cubes and the difference of two nth powers.

Difference of Two Squares

$$a^2 - b^2 = (a - b)(a + b)$$

Example: Factor $x^2 - 16$

$$x^2 - 16 = x^2 - 4^2$$

$$= (x - 4)(x + 4)$$

Difference of Two Cubes

$$a^3 - b^3 = (a - b)(a^2 + ab + b^2)$$

Example: Factor $8x^3 - 27$

$$8x^3 - 27 = (2x)^3 - 3^3$$

$$= (2x - 3)(4x^2 + 6x + 9)$$

Lesson Five: Polynomials and Rational Expressions (cont.)

Sum of Two Cubes

$$a^3 + b^3 = (a + b)(a^2 - ab + b^2)$$

Example: Factor $8x^3 + 27$

$$8x^3 + 27 = (2x)^3 + 3^3$$

$$= (2x + 3)(4x^2 - 6x + 9)$$

Difference of Two nth Powers

$$a^n - b^n = (a - b)(a^{n-1} + a^{n-2}b + a^{n-3}b^2 + \ldots + a^2b^{n-3} + ab^{n-2} + b^{n-1})$$

Example: Factor $81x^4 - 16$

$$81x^4 - 16 = (3x)^4 - 2^4$$

$$= (3x - 2)((3x)^3 + (3x)^2 2 + (3x)2^2 + 2^3)$$

$$= (3x - 2)(27x^3 + 18x^2 + 12x + 8)$$

Factoring can also be done by grouping. **Grouping** is the process of splitting up a long polynomial into groups of terms, each of which is factorable. The following examples show how this can be done.

Example: Factor $x^3 + 2x^2 + 5x + 10$

$$x^3 + 2x^2 + 5x + 10 = (x^3 + 5x) + (2x^2 + 10)$$

$$= x(x^2 + 5) + 2(x^2 + 5)$$

$$= (x + 2)(x^2 + 5)$$

Example: Factor $x^3 + x^2 - 4x - 64$

$$x^3 + x^2 - 4x - 64 = (x^3 - 64) + (x^2 - 4x)$$

$$= (x - 4)(x^2 + 4x + 16) + x(x - 4)$$

$$= (x - 4)(x^2 + 5x + 16)$$

The Factor Theorem can also be of use when you are trying to factor a tricky polynomial.

Factor Theorem

A polynomial $p(x)$ has a factor $(x - a)$, if and only if $p(a) = 0$.

You can test for linear factors by plugging in a particular value and checking whether or not the polynomial evaluates to zero. We will revisit this theorem in Lesson Nine when we are graphing functions and finding roots.

Lesson Five: Polynomials and Rational Expressions (cont.)

PARTIAL FRACTION DECOMPOSITION

A polynomial fraction whose denominator is of higher degree than its numerator can sometimes be broken into a sum of fractions called **partial fractions**. This operation is called **partial fraction decomposition**. It can be done when the denominator of the original polynomial fraction can be factored.

We will first consider the case where the denominator of the polynomial fraction can be factored into linear terms. The polynomial fraction can be represented as a sum of fractions, each containing a constant divided by one of the factors in the denominator of the polynomial fraction.

Example: Decompose the fraction $\dfrac{3x^2 + x - 20}{x^3 - 6x^2 + 11x - 6}$ into partial fractions.

1)   First, factor the denominator.

$$\frac{3x^2 + x - 20}{x^3 - 6x^2 + 11x - 6} = \frac{3x^2 + x - 20}{(x - 1)(x - 2)(x - 3)}$$

2)   Then, set the original fraction equal to the sum of three fractions. The denominator of each of the fractions is one of the factors of the denominator of the original fraction. The letters **A**, **B**, and **C** stand for numbers that we will need to find.

$$\frac{3x^2 + x - 20}{(x - 1)(x - 2)(x - 3)} = \frac{A}{x - 1} + \frac{B}{x - 2} + \frac{C}{x - 3}$$

3)   Multiply both sides of the equation by the denominator of the left-hand side.

$$\frac{(3x^2 + x - 20)(x - 1)(x - 2)(x - 3)}{(x - 1)(x - 2)(x - 3)} = \frac{A(x - 1)(x - 2)(x - 3)}{x - 1} + \frac{B(x - 1)(x - 2)(x - 3)}{x - 2} + \frac{C(x - 1)(x - 2)(x - 3)}{x - 3}$$

$$3x^2 + x - 20 = A(x - 2)(x - 3) + B(x - 1)(x - 3) + C(x - 1)(x - 2)$$

$$= A(x^2 - 5x + 6) + B(x^2 - 4x + 3) + C(x^2 - 3x + 2)$$

Lesson Five: Polynomials and Rational Expressions (cont.)

4) To find each of the **A**, **B**, and **C** values, set x to the value that would make its denominator zero.

To find **A**, set $x = 1$.

$$3(1^2) + 1 - 20 = A(1^2 - 5(1) + 6) + B(1^2 - 4(1) + 3) + C(1^2 - 3(1) + 2)$$

$$-16 = 2A + 0B + 0C$$

$$A = -8$$

To find **B**, set $x = 2$.

$$3(2^2) + 2 - 20 = A(2^2 - 5(2) + 6) + B(2^2 - 4(2) + 3) + C(2^2 - 3(2) + 2)$$

$$-6 = 0A - 1B + 0C$$

$$B = 6$$

To find **C**, set $x = 3$.

$$3(3^2) + 3 - 20 = A(3^2 - 5(3) + 6) + B(3^2 - 4(3) + 3) + C(3^2 - 3(3) + 2)$$

$$10 = 0A + 0B + 2C$$

$$C = 5$$

The polynomial fraction can now be represented by the sum of the following three fractions.

$$\frac{-8}{x-1} + \frac{6}{x-2} + \frac{5}{x-3}$$

Note: In order to decompose a polynomial fraction, the original fraction must have a numerator of lower degree than the denominator. If this is not the case, then you need to divide the denominator into the numerator. You can then represent the original fraction by the quotient, plus the remainder divided by the denominator of the original fraction. If necessary, you can decompose the remainder portion into partial fractions.

Lesson Five: Polynomials and Rational Expressions (cont.)

RATIONAL EXPRESSIONS

Expressions that can be written as one polynomial divided by another polynomial are called **rational expressions**. These expressions are important because they can be manipulated like ordinary rational numbers. The following examples show how rational expressions can be manipulated. In all cases, the manipulation results in a simpler expression.

Reducing Fractions

Rational fractions can be simplified by dividing the numerator and denominator by a common factor.

Example: Reduce the fraction $\dfrac{x^2 + 5x + 6}{2x^2 + 6x}$

$$\frac{x^2 + 5x + 6}{2x^2 + 6x} = \frac{(x + 2)(x + 3)}{2x(x + 3)}$$

$$= \frac{x + 2}{2x}$$

Multiplying Fractions

Rational expressions can be multiplied, and the resulting expression can often be simplified.

Example: Multiply the following $\dfrac{x + 3}{x^2 - 3x + 2} \cdot \dfrac{x^2 - x - 2}{3x^2 + 9x}$

$$\frac{x + 3}{x^2 - 3x + 2} \cdot \frac{x^2 - x - 2}{3x^2 + 9x} = \frac{x + 3}{(x - 1)(x - 2)} \cdot \frac{(x + 1)(x - 2)}{3x(x + 3)}$$

$$= \frac{1}{x - 1} \cdot \frac{x + 1}{3x} = \frac{x + 1}{3x^2 - 3x}$$

Lesson Five: Polynomials and Rational Expressions (cont.)

Dividing Fractions

Rational expressions can be divided, and the resulting expression can be simplified.

Example: Divide $\dfrac{x^2 - 5x + 6}{x + 1}$ by $\dfrac{x^2 - 4x + 3}{x^2 + 2x + 1}$

We divide by inverting the divisor and multiplying the inverted divisor times the dividend.

$$\dfrac{\dfrac{x^2 - 5x + 6}{x + 1}}{\dfrac{x^2 - 4x + 3}{x^2 + 2x + 1}} = \dfrac{x^2 - 5x + 6}{x + 1} \cdot \dfrac{x^2 + 2x + 1}{x^2 - 4x + 3}$$

$$= \dfrac{(x - 2)(x - 3)}{x + 1} \cdot \dfrac{(x + 1)^2}{(x - 1)(x - 3)}$$

$$= \dfrac{x - 2}{1} \cdot \dfrac{x + 1}{x - 1}$$

$$= \dfrac{x^2 - x - 2}{x - 1}$$

Adding or Subtracting Fractions With the Same Denominator

Rational expressions with the same denominator can easily be added or subtracted, and the resulting expression can often be simplified.

Example: Find $\dfrac{x}{x^2 - 3x + 2}$ minus $\dfrac{1}{x^2 - 3x + 2}$

$$\dfrac{x}{x^2 - 3x + 2} - \dfrac{1}{x^2 - 3x + 2} = \dfrac{x - 1}{x^2 - 3x + 2} = \dfrac{x - 1}{(x - 1)(x - 2)}$$

$$= \dfrac{1}{x - 2}$$

Lesson Five: Polynomials and Rational Expressions (cont.)

Adding or Subtracting Fractions With Different Denominators

Rational expressions with different denominators can be added or subtracted by placing each expression over a common denominator. The resulting expression can often be simplified.

Example: Find $\dfrac{3x}{x+1}$ plus $\dfrac{2x}{x-1}$

$$\dfrac{3x}{x+1} + \dfrac{2x}{x-1} = \dfrac{3x(x-1)}{(x+1)(x-1)} + \dfrac{2x(x+1)}{(x+1)(x-1)}$$

$$= \dfrac{3x^2 - 3x}{x^2 - 1} + \dfrac{2x^2 + 2x}{x^2 - 1}$$

$$= \dfrac{5x^2 - x}{x^2 - 1}$$

Name: _____ Date: _____

Lesson Five: Exercises

Complete the following exercises on your own paper.

1. Identify the following polynomials as monomials, binomials, or trinomials.

    a) $y = x^2 - 3x + 1$ **b)** $y = x^3 - 8$ **c)** $y = 6x^2$

    d) $y = -5x^3 - 2x - 1$ **e)** $y = -2x$ **f)** $y = 2x^2 - 5$

2. Rewrite the following polynomials so that they are in standard form (in descending powers of the variable).

    a) $y = 6x - 4x^4 - 2 + x^2 + 7x^3$ **b)** $y = 5 - x + 6x^3 - 11x^2$

    c) $y = 3x^2 - 11 + 4x^5 - 3x^3$ **d)** $y = 14 - 6x + 2x^3$

3. Find the values of the following quantities to the zero power.

    a) 1^0 **b)** 15^0 **c)** $10,000^0$ **d)** x^0

4. Find the sum or difference of the following pairs of polynomials.

    a) $2x^2 - 3x + 2$ plus $x^2 + 4x + 7$

    b) $4x^2 + 2x + 5$ minus $2x^2 - 3x + 3$

    c) $3x^3 + 2x^2 - 4x + 6$ plus $2x^3 - x^2 + 3x - 2$

    d) $5x^3 - 6x^2 - x - 3$ minus $4x^3 + 2x^2 - 3x + 1$

    e) $2x^4 + 3x^2 - 14$ plus $x^4 - 2x^3 + x$

    f) $3x^4 - 4x + 21$ minus $2x^3 + 3x^2 + 2x + 10$

    g) $2x^4 + 3x^3 + 6x^2 - 2x + 5$ plus $x^4 - 3x^2 + 4x$

    h) $5x^5 + 3x^4 + 2x^2 + 7x$ minus $2x^5 + 3x^4 - 4x^3 + 3x - 5$

5. Find the products of the following pairs of polynomials.

    a) $3x + 1$ times $2x - 5$

    b) $x - 2$ times $x + 7$

Lesson Five: Exercises (cont.)

c) $2x^2 - 3x + 1$ times $3x + 4$

d) $x^2 + x + 2$ times $x + 3$

e) $x^2 - 2x - 1$ times $2x^2 + 3x - 2$

f) $3x^2 + 4x + 8$ times $4x^2 - 2x + 3$

g) $x^3 - 2x + 3$ times $2x^3 + x^2 - 4$

h) $x^4 + 3x^3 - 2x^2 + 4x + 1$ times $2x^3 + 4x^2 - 6x + 3$

6. Find the following polynomial quotients.

a) $x^2 - 4x - 21$ divided by $x - 7$

b) $x^2 + x - 20$ divided by $x + 5$

c) $2x^4 + 11x^3 + 11x^2 - 3x + 4$ divided by $x + 4$

d) $x^4 - x^2 + 7x + 2$ divided by $x + 2$

e) $x^4 - 4x^3 + 5x^2 - 5x - 3$ divided by $x^3 - x^2 + 2x + 1$

f) $x^5 + 3x^4 - 2x^2 + 3x - 1$ divided by $x^2 + 2x - 1$

g) $x^6 - 3x^5 + 4x^4 - 7x^3 + 2x^2$ divided by x^2

h) $27x^5 + 36x^4 - 18x^3$ divided by $3x^3$

7. Find the quotient and the remainder in each of the following polynomial divisions.

a) $3x^2 - 3x + 2$ divided by $x + 1$

b) $x^3 + 4x^2 - 3x + 7$ divided by $x - 2$

c) $x^3 - 3x + 4$ divided by $x^2 - 2x + 1$

d) $x^4 + 3x^3 - x^2 + 2x + 6$ divided by $x^2 + x - 2$

Name: _____ Date: _____

Lesson Five: Exercises (cont.)

8. Factor the following polynomials using any method that you feel is appropriate.

a) $x^2 - 4$ **b)** $4x^2 - 9$ **c)** $8x^3 - 125$

d) $27x^3 + 64$ **e)** $x^3 - 216$ **f)** $x^6 - 64$

g) $32x^5 - 243$ **h)** $x^2 + 6x + 9$ **i)** $x^2 - 10x + 25$

j) $x^2 - x - 20$ **k)** $x^2 + 12x + 35$ **l)** $x^3 + 3x^2 + 9x + 27$

m) $x^3 + 4x^2 - 4x - 16$ **n)** $x^3 + 6x^2 + 11x + 6$ **o)** $9x^3 - 42x^2 + 49x$

p) $6x^3 + 17x^2 + 11x + 2$ **q)** $x^4 - 6x^3 + 9x^2$ **r)** $x^3 + 2x^2 - x - 2$

s) $x^4 - 1$

9. Decompose the following polynomial fractions into partial fractions.

a) $\dfrac{8x + 25}{x^2 + 7x + 10}$ **b)** $\dfrac{2x - 10}{x^2 - 10x + 21}$

c) $\dfrac{12x - 7}{6x^2 - 7x + 2}$ **d)** $\dfrac{2x^2 + 7x + 3}{x^3 + 2x^2 - x - 2}$

e) $\dfrac{5x^2 + 9x - 56}{x^3 - 5x^2 + 2x + 8}$ **f)** $\dfrac{8x - 2}{x^3 + x^2 - 2x}$

10. The following fractions have numerators of equal or higher degree than their denominators. Divide the numerator by the denominator and write the result as a quotient and a remainder divided by the denominator of the original fraction. Then, decompose the remainder fraction into partial fractions. Part a) is partially worked out for you.

a) $\dfrac{2x^3 - 6x^2 + 5x - 3}{x^2 - 3x + 2}$

$$
\begin{array}{r}
2x \\
x^2 - 3x + 2 \overline{)\, 2x^3 - 6x^2 + 5x - 3} \\
\underline{2x^3 - 6x^2 + 4x} \\
x - 3
\end{array}
$$

This fraction is equal to

$2x + \dfrac{x - 3}{x^2 - 3x + 2}$

Decompose the $\dfrac{x - 3}{x^2 - 3x + 2}$ part into partial fractions.

Name: _____ Date: _____

Lesson Five: Exercises (cont.)

Now try two more problems like this.

b) $\dfrac{2x^2 - 12}{x^2 - 4}$

c) $\dfrac{2x^3 + 3x^2 - x + 16}{x^2 + 2x - 3}$

11. Simplify the following rational expressions.

a) $\dfrac{x^2 - 4x + 4}{x^2 - x - 2}$

b) $\dfrac{x - 1}{x^2 - 1}$

c) $\dfrac{x - 3}{x^2 - 10x + 25} \cdot \dfrac{x - 5}{x^2 - 4x + 3}$

d) $\dfrac{x^2 - x - 30}{x - 1} \cdot \dfrac{x^2 - 2x + 1}{x^2 + 4x - 5}$

e) $\dfrac{x + 4}{x^2 + 6x + 9} \div \dfrac{x^2 + 9x + 20}{x + 3}$

f) $\dfrac{x - 2}{3x + 3} \div \dfrac{x^2 + 2x}{x + 2}$

g) $\dfrac{2x + 3}{x^2 + 3x + 2} - \dfrac{x + 1}{x^2 + 3x + 2}$

h) $\dfrac{x + 7}{x^2 + x - 20} + \dfrac{x + 3}{x^2 + x - 20}$

i) $\dfrac{3x - 3}{2x^2 - x - 1} + \dfrac{1}{2x + 1}$

j) $\dfrac{x}{x + 1} + \dfrac{x}{x - 1}$

Lesson Six: Exponentials and Logarithms

Trang was reading an article for his geography class when he saw a section about a very poor country. The article stated that the population of this country was increasing exponentially, but their food supply was only increasing linearly. There were graphs that showed the population and the amount of food produced in the last few years. It was obvious that the population was going up much faster than the food production. However, Trang was still not sure that he understood the ideas of exponential and linear increases, so he asked his teacher to explain.

"It is really quite simple," his teacher replied. "When something increases linearly with time, it increases by the same amount in each time period. The number of students in my class has been increasing linearly for the last four years. Each year there are two more students."

"When something increases exponentially," she continued, "the amount in the next time period is some number times the amount in the previous one. For example, if each year I had twice as many students in my class as in the previous year, the number of students would be increasing exponentially."

"Wow," replied Trang. "There is a big difference between a linear and an exponential increase."

EXPONENTIAL FUNCTIONS

An **exponential function** is one that has a variable as the exponent or power of some number. The power is simply called the **exponent**, and the number is called the **base**. In the exponential function $y = 2^x$, the base is **2** and the exponent is **x**. The following are exponential functions.

$$f(x) = 2^x \qquad\qquad f(x) = 3^{-x} \qquad\qquad f(x) = 4 \cdot 3^{2x}$$

$$f(q) = 2.5^q \qquad\qquad f(z) = 5.5 \cdot 3.5^z$$

The domain of an exponential function is the real numbers. In other words, an exponential function is defined for all real values of the variable. The range of the function, however, is limited to the positive real numbers if the base is a positive number. Some function values, using the function $f(x) = 2^x$, are shown in the example below.

Evaluate $f(x) = 2^x$ at $x = 0$, $x = 1$, $x = 2$, and $x = -2$.

$f(0) = 2^0 = 1$ $\qquad\qquad$ (Anything to the zero power is 1)

$f(1) = 2^1 = 2$

$f(2) = 2^2 = 4$

$f(-2) = 2^{-2} = \frac{1}{2^2} = \frac{1}{4}$

Lesson Six: Exponentials and Logarithms (cont.)

Notice that a number to a negative power is equal to one divided by the number to the positive power.

$$a^{-x} = \frac{1}{a^x}$$

In the examples above, we have shown only integer values of the exponent variable. The variable, however, can be any real number, even one with a fractional part. The other values in the function can also be real numbers. The general form of an exponential function can be written as:

$$f(x) = a \cdot b^{cx} \quad \text{where } a, b, \text{ and } c \text{ are real numbers, and } x \text{ is a real variable.}$$

To calculate values of exponential functions with fractional values for the exponent variable, you will need to use the "**x to the y**" function on your calculator. Your teacher will show you how to use it. Practice by finding values of $f(x)$ for indicated values of **x** in the example below.

Evaluate $f(x) = 1.80 \cdot 2.50^x$ for $x = 1.5$, $x = 3.6$, and $x = -2.75$.

$$f(x) = 1.80 \cdot 2.50^{1.5} = 1.80(3.95) = 7.11$$

$$f(x) = 1.80 \cdot 2.50^{3.6} = 1.80(27.08) = 48.74$$

$$f(x) = 1.80 \cdot 2.50^{-2.75} = 1.80(0.0805) = 0.15$$

GRAPHING EXPONENTIAL FUNCTIONS

Graphs of exponential functions are easy to produce. The values of the variable plotted on the vertical axis become large, however, so the graph needs to be limited to a specific portion of the domain. Graphs of $y = 2^x$ and $y = 2^{-x}$ are shown below and on the next page.

$y = 2^x$

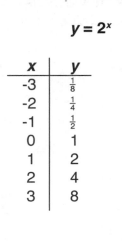

x	y
-3	$\frac{1}{8}$
-2	$\frac{1}{4}$
-1	$\frac{1}{2}$
0	1
1	2
2	4
3	8

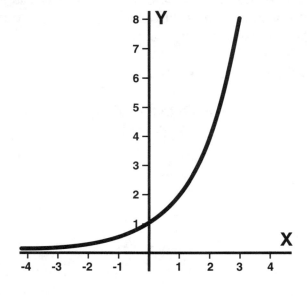

Lesson Six: Exponentials and Logarithms (cont.)

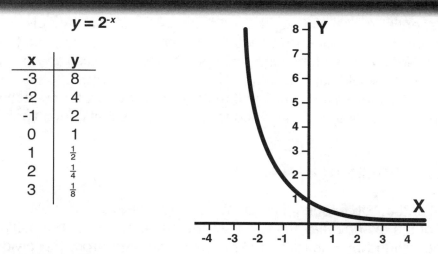

$y = 2^{-x}$

x	y
-3	8
-2	4
-1	2
0	1
1	$\frac{1}{2}$
2	$\frac{1}{4}$
3	$\frac{1}{8}$

Notice that the value of **y** in the graph of $y = 2^x$ gets large very quickly as **x** gets large in the positive direction. As **x** gets more and more negative, however, the value of **y** approaches but never reaches the x-axis. We sometimes say that the **limit** of **y** as **x** goes to negative infinity is 0.

The graph of $y = 2^{-x}$ is much like the $y = 2^x$ graph, except that it appears to be reversed with respect to the y-axis. As **x** becomes more negative, **y** becomes large, and as **x** becomes more and more positive, **y** approaches, but never reaches, the x-axis. In this case, the **limit** of **y** as **x** goes to positive infinity is 0.

It is possible to shift an exponential function upward or downward along the y-axis by adding a positive or negative constant to it. For example, the function $y = 2^x + 1$ would have the same shape as $y = 2^x$ but would cross the vertical axis at $y = 2$ instead of $y = 1$. The **limit** of **y** as **x** went to negative infinity would be 1 instead of 0.

It is also possible to shift an exponential function horizontally along the x-axis by adding or subtracting a constant to or from the exponential variable. The function $y = 2^{x-2}$ would evaluate to 1 at $x = 2$ instead of $x = 0$, and the function $y = 2^{x+1}$ would evaluate to 1 at $x = -1$. The graph below shows $y = 2^x + 1$, and $y = 2^{x-2}$. Notice that the curves all have the same basic shape. Only their positions on the coordinate axes are different.

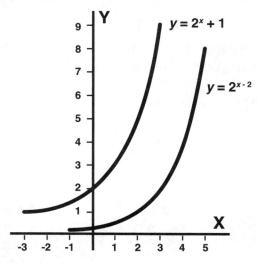

$y = 2^x + 1$

$y = 2^{x-2}$

Lesson Six: Exponentials and Logarithms (cont.)

The shape of the exponential curve can be changed somewhat if the variable in the exponent is multiplied by a constant. The function $y = 2^{2x}$ would be steeper than $y = 2^x$, and $y = 2^{x/2}$ would not be as steep as $y = 2^x$. Both of these functions would still cross the y-axis at $y = 1$, and the limit as x went to negative infinity would still be 0.

Finally, it is possible to have exponential functions that have x^2 or even x terms to higher powers as their exponents. We will be concerned with exponential functions that contain only the first power of x.

MULTIPLYING AND DIVIDING EXPONENTIAL FUNCTIONS

It is possible to multiply and divide exponential functions, and it is even possible to take them to a power. If the bases of the exponential functions are the same, they can be multiplied by adding their exponents and divided by subtracting the divisor exponent from the dividend exponent.

$$a^{x1} \cdot a^{x2} = a^{x1 + x2}$$

$$\frac{a^{x1}}{a^{x2}} = a^{x1 - x2}$$

Examples:

$$2^{2x} \cdot 2^x = 2^{2x + x} = 2^{3x}$$

$$4^{-3x} \cdot 4^{2x + 1} = 4^{-3x + 2x + 1} = 4^{-x + 1}$$

$$\frac{3^{5x}}{3^{2x}} = 3^{5x - 2x} = 3^{3x}$$

$$\frac{5^{2x + 1}}{5^{x - 2}} = 5^{2x + 1 - (x - 2)} = 5^{x + 3}$$

If the exponentials are multiplied by real number constants, the constants can be multiplied or divided and the exponents added or subtracted. The examples below show how this is done.

$$4 \cdot 2^x \cdot 8 \cdot 2^{2x} = (4)(8) \cdot 2^{x + 2x} = 32 \cdot 2^{3x}$$

$$\frac{8 \cdot 2^{2x}}{4 \cdot 2^x} = \frac{8}{4} \cdot 2^{2x - x} = 2 \cdot 2^x$$

Lesson Six: Exponentials and Logarithms (cont.)

The multiplication and division rules can be used to change the appearance of an exponential function (without changing its values). The two examples below show some handy manipulations.

$$4 \cdot 2^x = 2^2 \cdot 2^x = 2^{x+2}$$

$$\tfrac{1}{4} \cdot 2^x = \frac{2^x}{2^2} = 2^{x-2}$$

Exponentials can also be taken to a power. The rule for doing this is shown below.

$$(a^x)^b = a^{bx}$$

Examples:

$$(2^x)^4 = 2^{4x}$$

$$(3^{2x})^5 = 3^{5 \cdot 2x} = 3^{10x}$$

$$(2^{4x})^{3/2} = 2^{3/2 \cdot 4x} = 2^{6x}$$ (Remember - a quantity to the *m/n* power is the *n*th root of the quantity to the *m* power.)

$$4^2(4^{2x})^3 = 4^2(4^{3 \cdot 2x}) = 4^2 \cdot 4^{6x} = 4^{6x+2}$$ (Do the power first.)

THE IRRATIONAL NUMBER *e*

The quantity, denoted by the symbol *e*, has special significance in mathematics. It is an irrational number that is the base of natural logarithms (introduced in the last section of this lesson), and it is often seen in practical problems that involve natural exponential growth or decay. The value of *e* (approximated) is shown below.

e = 2.7182818284...

You can reproduce this value by finding e^1 on your calculator; just enter 1 and then activate the e^x (sometimes called **exp**) feature.

Functions of the form $y = Ce^{kx}$ or $y = Ce^{-kx}$ (where *C* and *k* are real number constants) are often of interest, especially in science and engineering problems.

Lesson Six: Exponentials and Logarithms (cont.)

LOGARITHMS

A **logarithm** is the power to which some fixed number, called a **base**, must be raised in order to obtain a specified number. Logarithms of specified numbers will have different values, depending on which base is used. The three most commonly used bases are **2**, **10**, and **e**.

It is sometimes easiest (initially, at least) to look at logarithms in exponential forms. Consider the exponential function below.

$$x = a^y$$

In this equation, **a** taken to the **y** power gives **x**. We say that **a** is the base and **y** is the logarithm of **x**. This equation can be written in a different way.

$$y = \log_a x$$

This form of the equation says that **y** is the logarithm to the base **a** of **x**.

Examples:

1) Find the logarithm to the base 2 of 16.

   Since $2^4 = 16$, the logarithm of 16 to the base 2 is 4.

2) Find the logarithm to the base 4 of 16.

   Since $4^2 = 16$, the logarithm of 16 to the base 4 is 2.

3) Find the logarithm to the base 3 of 81.

   Since $3^4 = 81$, the logarithm of 81 to the base 3 is 4.

4) Find the logarithm to the base 10 of 1,000.

   Since $10^3 = 1,000$, the logarithm of 1,000 to the base 10 is 3.

5) Find the logarithm to the base 10 of 100.

   Since $10^2 = 100$, the logarithm of 100 to the base 10 is 2.

6) Find the logarithm to the base 10 of 1.

   Since $10^0 = 1$, the logarithm of 1 to the base 10 is 0.

Lesson Six: Exponentials and Logarithms (cont.)

The logarithms found in the examples on the previous page could be written in the following forms:

1) $4 = \log_2 16$ 2) $2 = \log_4 16$

3) $4 = \log_3 81$ 4) $3 = \log_{10} 1{,}000$

5) $2 = \log_{10} 100$ 6) $0 = \log_{10} 1$

The logarithms in the examples all turned out to be integers. This is not always the case. A logarithm can be any real number. The number that the logarithm represents, however, must be a positive real number. We can say this differently as follows:

The domain of $y = \log_a x$ is all positive real numbers, **x**. (The logarithm is not defined for **$x \leq 0$**.)

The range of $y = \log_a x$ is all real numbers, **y**.

Additional insight into the nature of logarithms can be gained by looking at a graph of **$y = \log_a x$**. Such a graph (for **$y = \log_2 x$**) is shown below.

$y = \log_2 x$

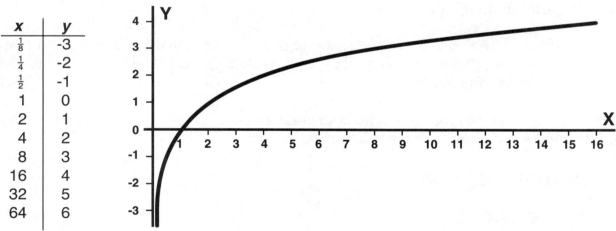

x	y
$\frac{1}{8}$	-3
$\frac{1}{4}$	-2
$\frac{1}{2}$	-1
1	0
2	1
4	2
8	3
16	4
32	5
64	6

Notice that the graph never crosses the y-axis. Notice also that the logarithm of 1 is zero, and that the logarithms of quantities that are less than 1 are negative. This is true for any base.

Lesson Six: Exponentials and Logarithms (cont.)

ANTILOGARITHMS

The inverse process of finding a logarithm is finding an **antilogarithm**. An antilogarithm (sometimes abbreviated **antilog**) is equal to the base to the logarithm power. In the equation $y = \log_a x$, y is the logarithm (to the base a) of x, and x is the antilogarithm (to the base a) of y. The antilogarithm can be found from the equation $x = a^y$.

Examples:

1)   Find the antilogarithm (to the base 2) of 4.

The antilog is $x = 2^4 = 16$

2)   Find the antilog (to the base 4) of 3.

The antilog is $x = 4^3 = 64$

3)   Find the antilog (to the base 10) of 5.

The antilog is $x = 10^5 = 100,000$

Rules for Manipulating Logarithms

There are three rules for manipulating logarithms of products, quotients, and powers of quantities. They are similar, in some ways, to the rules for manipulating exponents involving products, quotients, and powers.

If b and c are two real numbers, both greater than 0, p is a real number power (any real number), and a is a base, then the following rules hold.

$$\log_a (bc) = \log_a b + \log_a c$$

$$\log_a \frac{b}{c} = \log_a b - \log_a c$$

$$\log_a (b^p) = p \log_a b$$

Lesson Six: Exponentials and Logarithms (cont.)

Examples:

1) $\log_2 (6(x - 1)) = \log_2 6 + \log_2 (x - 1)$

2) $\log_{10} \dfrac{(x + 5)}{4} = \log_{10} (x + 5) - \log_{10} 4$

3) $\log_4 x^6 = 6 \log_4 x$

Common Logarithms

Logarithms to the base 10 are called **common logarithms**. They are often denoted as:

$y = \log x$

When no base is specified, it is understood that the base is 10.

You can find the common logarithm of a number on your calculator by entering the number and activating the **log** (or **log 10**) key. You can find the antilogarithm by entering the logarithm and activating the **10^x** (or **inverse log**) key.

Natural Logarithms

Logarithms to the base e are called **natural logarithms**. They are denoted as:

$y = \log_e x$ or $y = \ln x$

You can find the natural logarithm of a number on your calculator by entering the number and activating the **log$_e$** (or **ln**) key. You can get the antilogarithm by entering the natural logarithm and activating the **e^x** (or **inverse ln**) key.

Name: _____ Date: _____

Lesson Six: Exercises

Complete the following exercises on your own paper.

1. Plot the exponential functions $y = 4^x$ and $y = 3^{-x}$ on the same graph. Where does each of the graphs cross the y-axis? For what values do each of the graphs approach $y = 0$? Which of the two curves is the steepest?

2. Plot the exponential functions $y = 2^x$, $y = 2^{x-2}$, and $y = 2^{x+2}$ on the same graph. What can you say about the shape of the graph of each of the functions? Where is $y = 1$ for each of these functions?

3. Plot the exponential functions $y = 2^{-x}$, $y = 2^{-x} + 2$, and $y = 2^{-x} - 2$ on the same graph. What can you say about the shape of the graph of each of these functions? Where does each of your functions cross the y-axis?

4. Plot the exponential functions $y = 2^x$, $y = 2^{2x}$, and $y = 2^{4x}$ on the same graph. What can you say about the shape of the graph of each of these functions? Where does each of the graphs cross the y-axis? For what values do each of the graphs approach $y = 0$? Which of the curves is the steepest?

5. Use the e^x function on your calculator to plot e^x and e^{-x} on the same graph.

6. For $y = f(x) = 3^{2x+1}$, find $f(-1)$, $f(-\tfrac{1}{2})$, $f(0)$, $f(1)$, and $f(2)$.

7. Simplify the following exponential equations so that there are no products, quotients, or powers of exponentials (a and b are constants).

a) $y = 3^{2x} \cdot 3^{3x}$

b) $y = 3^{-2x} \cdot 3^{5x}$

c) $y = 2^{2x} \cdot 2^x \cdot 2^3$

d) $y = 2^{-3x} \cdot 2^{-x}$

e) $y = \dfrac{5^{3x}}{5^x}$

f) $y = \dfrac{3^{2x+4}}{3^3}$

g) $y = \dfrac{2^{-3x}}{2^{-5x}}$

h) $y = \dfrac{2^{3x+1}}{2^{4x-3}}$

i) $y = (4^x)^3$

j) $y = (2^2)^{4x}$

k) $y = 3^2 \cdot (3^{2x})^4$

l) $y = \dfrac{5^3 \cdot (5^2)^{5x}}{5^{x-1}}$

m) $y = a^{6x} \cdot a^{3x}$

n) $y = \dfrac{b^{5x}}{b^{2x}}$

o) $y = \dfrac{a^x}{a^{3x}}$

p) $y = (b^{2x})^3$

Lesson Six: Exercises (cont.)

8. The following problems contain bases to fractional powers. Simplify the given equations so that there are no products, quotients, or powers of exponentials. Two examples are shown below. (a and b are constants.)

$$y = 2^{\frac{2x}{5}} \cdot 2^{\frac{x}{5}}$$

$$= 2^{\left(\frac{2x}{5}+\frac{x}{5}\right)} = 2^{\frac{3x}{5}}$$

$$y = \frac{5^{\frac{5x}{2}}}{5^x}$$

$$= 5^{\left(\frac{5x}{2}-\frac{2x}{2}\right)} = 5^{\frac{3x}{2}}$$

a) $y = 3^{\frac{2x}{3}} \cdot 3^{\frac{x}{3}}$

b) $y = 5^{\frac{-5x}{2}} \cdot 5^{\frac{3x}{2}}$

c) $y = a^{\frac{-x}{2}} \cdot a^x$

d) $y = 7^{\frac{-x}{2}} \cdot 7^x \cdot 7^{\frac{3x}{2}}$

e) $y = \dfrac{2^{\frac{4x}{5}}}{2^{\frac{3x}{5}}}$

f) $y = \dfrac{3^{\frac{7x}{3}}}{3^{\frac{4x}{3}}}$

g) $y = \dfrac{5^{\frac{-x}{3}}}{5^{\frac{4x}{3}}}$

h) $y = \dfrac{a^{\frac{-3x}{2}}}{a^x}$

i) $y = \left(3^{\frac{x}{2}}\right)^3$

j) $y = \left(2^{\frac{-x}{3}}\right)^5$

k) $y = \left(b^{\frac{4x}{5}}\right)^2$

l) $y = \left(b^{\frac{-x}{2}}\right)^2$

9. Rationalize the denominators of the following equations so that there are no fractional powers in the denominators. Simplify the resulting expressions. An example is shown below. (a and b are constants.)

$$y = \frac{1 + a^{\frac{1}{2}}}{1 - a^{\frac{3}{2}}}$$

$$= \frac{(1 + a^{\frac{1}{2}})(1 + a^{\frac{3}{2}})}{(1 - a^{\frac{3}{2}})(1 + a^{\frac{3}{2}})} = \frac{1 + a^{\frac{1}{2}} + a^{\frac{3}{2}} + a^2}{1 - a^3}$$

a) $y = \dfrac{1 - 2^{\frac{x}{2}}}{1 + 2^{\frac{x}{2}}}$

Hint: Multiply numerator and denominator by $1 - 2^{\frac{x}{2}}$.

b) $y = \dfrac{2 + 2^{\frac{x}{2}}}{1 - 2^{\frac{x}{2}}}$

Hint: Multiply numerator and denominator by $1 + 2^{\frac{x}{2}}$.

Name: _____ Date: _____

Lesson Six: Exercises (cont.)

c) $y = \dfrac{a^x + a^{\frac{x}{2}}}{a^{\frac{x}{2}} + 1}$

Hint: Multiply numerator and denominator by $a^{\frac{x}{2}} - 1$.

d) $y = \dfrac{2^{\frac{3x}{2}} + 2^{\frac{x}{2}}}{1 - 2^{\frac{3x}{2}}}$

Hint: Multiply numerator and denominator by $1 + 2^{\frac{3x}{2}}$.

e) $y = \dfrac{1}{1 + a^{\frac{5x}{2}}}$

f) $y = \dfrac{b}{b - b^{\frac{x}{2}}}$

g) $y = \dfrac{3}{3^{\frac{3x}{2}} + 3^{\frac{x}{2}}}$

h) $y = \dfrac{1}{a^{\frac{x}{2}} - b^{\frac{3x}{2}}}$

10. Use your calculator to find e^2, $e^{1.5}$, e^{-2}, e^0, and $e^{5.5}$.

11. Simplify the following so that there are no products or powers in the exponentials.

a) $y = e^x \cdot e^{3x}$

b) $y = e^4 \cdot e^{5x}$

c) $y = \dfrac{e^{4x}}{e^{2x}}$

d) $y = \dfrac{e^{3x} \cdot e^{-x+4}}{e^{-x+2}}$

e) $y = (e^{2x})^3$

f) $y = \dfrac{e^2 \cdot (e^3)^{4x}}{e^{x+1}}$

12. Find the logarithms (to the indicated bases) of the following numbers.

a) $\log_2 8$

b) $\log_3 243$

c) $\log_{10} 100{,}000$

d) $\log_4 64$

e) $\log_3 \frac{1}{9}$

f) $\log_2 \frac{1}{16}$

g) $\log_{10} 10$

h) $\log_7 49$

i) $\log_5 125$

j) $\log_{10} \frac{1}{100}$

k) $\log_2 512$

l) $\log_2 128$

13. Plot the logarithmic functions $y = \log x$ (base 10) and $y = \ln x$ (base e) on the same graph. Use your calculator to find the logarithm values. Where do both of your plots cross the x-axis? Do either of your plots cross the y-axis? For both of your plots, what is the limit as x gets closer and closer to 0?

Name: _____ Date: _____

Lesson Six: Exercises (cont.)

14. Find the antilogs (to the specified base) of the following logarithm values.

a) 3 (base 2)

b) -2 (base 2)

c) 4 (base 3)

d) -1 (base 3)

e) 0 (base 4)

f) 2 (base 4)

g) 4 (base 10)

h) -1 (base 10)

15. Simplify the following equations by writing the log term as a sum or difference of two or more other log terms.

a) $y = \log_2 (4x)$

b) $y = \log_4 (x - 1)(x + 10)$

c) $y = \log_{10} \dfrac{x + 5}{x}$

d) $y = \log_e \dfrac{x}{10}$

e) $y = \log_3 \dfrac{5x}{2}$

f) $y = \log_5 \left(x \dfrac{x + 1}{2} \right)$

16. Combine the following sums and differences of log terms into single log terms involving products or quotients.

a) $y = \log_5 x + \log_5 (x + 5)$

b) $y = \log_e 6 + \log_e (2x)$

c) $y = \log_3 x - \log_3 4$

d) $y = \log_{10} x - \log_{10} (x - 1)$

e) $y = \log_2 3 + \log_2 4 + \log_2 x$

f) $y = \log_2 5 + \log_2 x - \log_2 3$

17. Simplify the following logarithmic equations so that there are no terms involving powers.

a) $y = \log_{10} x^4$

b) $y = \log_2 x^7$

c) $y = \log_3 x^{-5}$

d) $y = \log_e (2x)^3$

e) $y = \log_4 \left(\dfrac{x}{5} \right)^3$

f) $y = \log_2 \left(\dfrac{x^3}{5^2} \right)$

18. Use your calculator to find the following common (base 10) logarithms.

a) log 7.9   **b)** log 25   **c)** log 0.25   **d)** log 1,298 **e)** log 1

19. Use your calculator to find the antilogs of the following common (base 10) logarithms.

a) 3.78   **b)** 12   **c)** -9   **d)** -0.5   **e)** 0

20. Use your calculator to find the antilogs of the following natural (base e) logarithms.

a) ln 7.9   **b)** ln 25   **c)** ln 0.25   **d)** ln 1,298 **e)** ln 1

21. Use your calculator to find the following natural (base e) logarithms.

a) 3.78   **b)** 12   **c)** -9   **d)** -0.5   **e)** 0

Lesson Seven: Trigonometric Functions

Carlos was trying to set up a telescope for his science class. He was puzzled, however, by the measuring circles on the scope that were labeled azimuth and elevation. His friend, Rosa, came to his rescue.

"Those are angle settings," explained Rosa. "They allow you to measure the angle that the telescope is rotated from due north, and the angle that it is elevated, or tilted up, above the horizon."

"Now I see," replied Carlos. "The combination of these two angles tells you exactly where the telescope is pointed. This angle stuff that we learned in math class is really pretty useful."

ANGLES

There are many ways to describe angles. They can be measures of the amount of rotation of something, the difference in the directions of two intersecting lines, or portions of a circle. We will use the following definition of an angle.

*An **angle** is generated by the rotation of a line, in a plane, about one of the points on the line. The point about which the line is rotated is called the **vertex** of the angle.*

Angles are often given names that are Greek letters, such as α (alpha) , β (beta), δ (delta), γ (gamma), ϕ (phi), or θ (theta). The figure below shows several angles. In most cases, the rotation that produces the angle is in the counterclockwise direction.

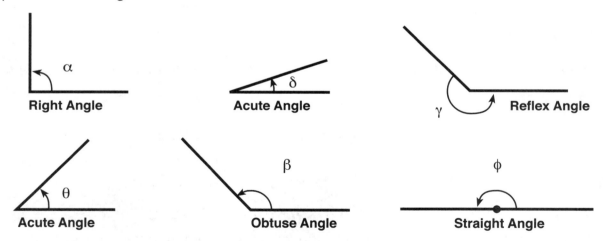

Angles are commonly measured in either **degrees** or **radians**. A **degree** is 1/360th of a complete rotation. It is often indicated by the symbol °. There are 360 degrees (360°) in a complete rotation (a circle). Angles can be measured **relatively** (e.g., the angle between two arbitrarily oriented lines), or **absolutely**, with respect to a fixed *x-y* coordinate system. In the latter case, an angle is measured in the counterclockwise direction from the positive *x*-axis. The positive *x*-axis is assumed to extend in the 0° direction.

One-fourth of a complete rotation generates a **90° angle**. A 90° angle is also called a **right angle**. Two lines that meet in a right angle are said to be **perpendicular**. One-half of a complete rotation generates a **180° angle**, also called a **straight angle**. An angle that

Lesson Seven: Trigonometric Functions (cont.)

is less than 90° is called an **acute angle**, one that is between 90° and 180° is called an **obtuse angle**, and one that is greater than 180°, but less than 360°, is called a **reflex angle**.

A **radian** is a much larger unit of angular measure than is a degree. It is often associated with the constant, π.

Remember: The value of π is approximately $\pi = 3.14159...$

A radian is $\frac{1}{2}\pi$ of a complete rotation. There are, therefore, 2π radians in a complete rotation and 2π radians in 360°. There are π radians in 180° and $\pi/2$ radians in 90°. The following formulas can be used to convert between radians and degrees.

$$1° = \pi/180 \text{ radians} \qquad\qquad 1 \text{ radian} = 180°/\pi$$
$$= 0.01745 \qquad\qquad\qquad\qquad\quad = 57.30°$$

Examples:

1)   Convert 65° to radians.

65° · 0.01745 radians/degree = 1.13 radians

2)   Convert 1.75 radians to degrees

1.75 radians · 57.30 degrees/radian = 100°

A radian can also be defined in terms of a circle. The figure shows a circle of radius, r, with an angle drawn in it. The angle has been chosen so that the distance that it marks off on the circumference of the circle is exactly equal to the radius of the circle. An angle of this size is equal to one radian.

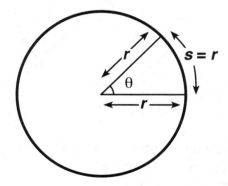

This definition of a radian can also be used to write a useful relation between an angle, θ, and the distance, s, that it marks off (**subtends**) on the circumference of a circle of radius, r.

$$s = r\theta$$

Lesson Seven: Trigonometric Functions (cont.)

In this equation, θ is in radians and **s** and **r** are in the same distance units. For a circle of radius, **r**, you can find θ if you know **s**, and you can find **s** if you know θ.

Examples:

1) The radius of a circle is 5 inches. An angle, θ, subtends a distance of 3 inches along the circumference of the circle. What is the angle?

$$\theta = \frac{s}{r} = \frac{3 \text{ inches}}{5 \text{ inches}} = 0.6 \text{ radians}$$

2) The radius of a circle is 10 centimeters. An angle of 1.25 radians subtends an arc of length **s** along the circumference of the circle. What is the length of the arc?

$$s = r\theta = 10 \text{ cm} \times 1.25 \text{ radians} = 12.5 \text{ cm}$$

TRIGONOMETRIC FUNCTIONS

Most practical applications of trigonometry use trigonometric functions. **Trigonometric functions** are functions that relate the measure of an angle to a ratio of real numbers.

The trigonometric functions are easiest to introduce from the unit circle, a circle centered at the origin with a radius of 1. Such a circle ($x^2 + y^2 = 1$) is shown in the figure below. The coordinate axes divide the circle into four regions. These regions are called **quadrants** and are numbered **I**, **II**, **III**, and **IV**, starting with the upper right one and proceeding counterclockwise to the lower right one.

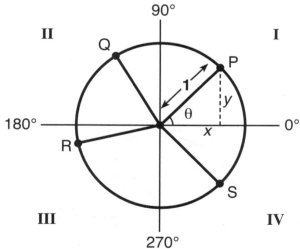

A point on the circle, such as the one labeled **P**, is at a distance of 1 unit from the origin. It has a horizontal coordinate, **x**, and a vertical coordinate, **y**. A line from the origin to the point **P** defines an angle, θ, with the positive x-axis.

We define the **sine** (abbreviated **sin**) of the angle, θ, to be

$$\sin \theta = \frac{y}{1} = y$$

Lesson Seven: Trigonometric Functions (cont.)

Another way of stating this is to define the sine in terms of the right triangle formed by the radius of the circle, the *x*-axis, and a perpendicular from point P to the *x*-axis. The sine of the angle θ is just the length of the side of the triangle opposite θ divided by the length of the hypotenuse of the triangle (1). The sine is a positive quantity when the angle is in quadrant I or quadrant II (points **P** and **Q** in the diagram), but it has a negative value when the angle is in quadrant III or IV (points **R** and **S** in the diagram).

If the sine function is plotted on the vertical axis of a graph, versus the angle on the horizontal, the following "sinusoidal" plot results. (NOTE: You can find the sine of an angle with your calculator. Just type in the angle, and then press the **sin** key. If your angle is in degrees, make sure the calculator is in the degree mode; if the angle is in radians, make sure the calculator is in the radians mode. Your instructor will show you how to set the mode.)

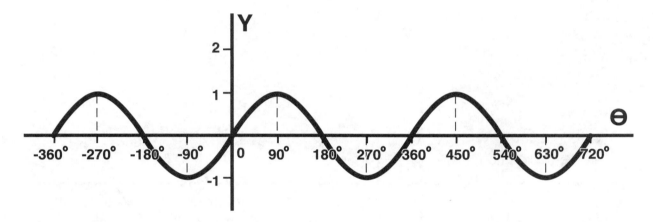

Notice that the sine is positive for angles between 0° and 180° and negative between 180° and 360°, and that it crosses the horizontal axis at 0°, 180°, 360°, etc. Notice also that its maximum value is 1, that its minimum value is -1, and that it repeats itself in 360° intervals. The maximum value is sometimes called the **amplitude**, and the 360° interval is called the **period**. The amplitude can be changed by multiplying the function times a constant. For example, the amplitude of **sin** θ is 1. The period can be changed by multiplying the angle times a constant. For example, the period of **sin 2θ** is 180°.

The graph of the sine function can be shifted to the left or the right by adding a constant to the angle. For example, **sin (θ - 10°)** would shift the sine curve 10° to the right and **sin (θ + 10°)** would shift it 10° to the left. The constant is sometimes called a **phase**.

Lesson Seven: Trigonometric Functions (cont.)

Another trigonometric function is called the **cosine** (abbreviated **cos**). Like the sine, the cosine can be defined from the unit circle in the diagram on page 70.

$$\cos \theta = \frac{x}{1} = x$$

In terms of the triangle formed by the radius of the circle, the x-axis, and a perpendicular from **P** to the x-axis, the cosine is equal to the side adjacent to the angle divided by the hypotenuse (1). A graph of the cosine function looks like a graph of the sine function shifted by 90°. Its amplitude is 1 and its period is 360°. The cosine is 1 when the angle is 0°. (NOTE: You can find cosine values on your calculator by entering the angle and pressing the **cos** key.)

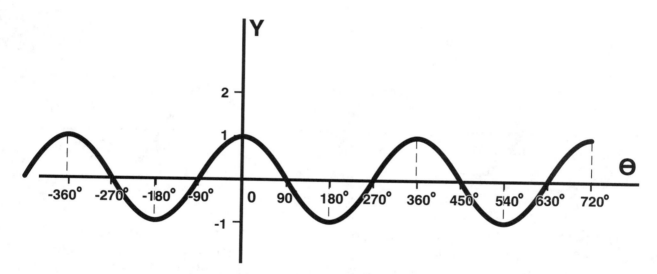

The amplitude of the cosine function can be changed by multiplying the function times a constant, and the period can be changed by multiplying the angle times a constant. Also, like the sine function, the cosine function can be shifted to the left or the right by adding an appropriate constant to the angle.

Lesson Seven: Trigonometric Functions (cont.)

Yet another trig function is called the **tangent** (abbreviated **tan**). On the unit circle, it can be defined as the side opposite the angle θ (**y**) divided by the side adjacent to the angle θ (**x**). (NOTE: You can find tangent values on your calculator by entering an angle and then pressing the **tan** key.)

$$\tan \theta = \frac{y}{x}$$

The tangent can also be expressed as the sine of the angle divided by the cosine of the angle.

$$\tan \theta = \frac{\sin \theta}{\cos \theta}$$

The graph of the tangent function looks much different from that of the sine and the cosine. The tangent goes to 0 at angles where the sine goes to 0 and approaches infinity as the angle approaches values where the cosine goes to 0.

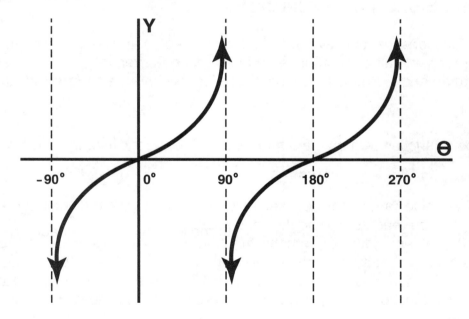

There are three other trigonometric functions, the **cosecant (csc)**, the **secant (sec)**, and the **cotangent (cot)**. They can be defined as the inverses of the sine, the cosine, and the tangent.

$$\csc \theta = \frac{1}{\sin \theta} \qquad \sec \theta = \frac{1}{\cos \theta} \qquad \cot \theta = \frac{1}{\tan \theta}$$

Lesson Seven: Trigonometric Functions (cont.)

A TRIGONOMETRIC IDENTITY

The sine and the cosine of an angle are related in an interesting way. If you look at the diagram that contains the unit circle, you will see a triangle defined by point **P**, the origin, and the point where the perpendicular from **P** meets the x-axis. The two short sides of the triangle have lengths, *x* and *y*, and the hypotenuse is of length 1. The Pythagorean Theorum tells us that

$$x^2 + y^2 = 1$$

Substituting in the definitions of the sine and the cosine gives the following equation, called a **trigonometric identity**.

$$\sin^2 \theta + \cos^2 \theta = 1$$

This identity is true for any value of θ and shows that the sine and cosine of an angle are related. This is just one example of a trigonometric identity. There are many others.

THE INVERSE TRIGONOMETRIC FUNCTIONS

The trig functions that we have been looking at take an angle as an argument and return a sine, cosine, or tangent value. Another set of functions, however, take a sine, cosine, or tangent value and return an angle. These functions are called the **inverse trigonometric functions**.

Arcsin

The **arcsin** function returns the angle whose sine is specified. It is written as

arcsin *s*,

where *s* is a sine value (a number between -1 and 1). It is sometimes called the **inverse sine** function, and it is often read as "the angle whose sine is" *s*.

There is a problem, however, with this function. The sine function is not one-to-one. Many different angles can give the same sine value. For example, the sine of 90° is 1, but so is the sine of -270° and 450°. For this reason, the domain of the function is usually restricted to between -90° and 90°. The arcsin function is written with an uppercase "A" to indicate the restricted domain.

Arcsin *s*

(NOTE: You can find Arcsin values on your calculator. Enter a sine value and then activate the inverse sin. You may have to press the **inv** or **2nd** key and then press the **sin** key. Your calculator will return the angle in the restricted domain in radians or in degrees, depending on which mode you have set.)

Example: Find the angle whose sine is 0.5.

θ = Arcsin 0.5 = 30°

Lesson Seven: Trigonometric Functions (cont.)

Arccos

The **arccos** function returns "the angle whose cosine is" the specified value. It is sometimes called the **inverse cosine**. Like the arcsin, it is restricted to a certain domain, in this case, from 0° to 180°, and written with an uppercase "A."

Arccos *c*

The *c* indicates a cosine value (between -1 and 1). (NOTE: You can use your calculator to find Arccos values. Enter a cosine value and then activate the inverse cosine function. Your calculator will return the angle in the restricted domain.)

Example: Find the angle whose cosine is 0.5.

$$\theta = \textbf{Arccos } 0.5 = 60°$$

Arctan

The **Arctan** (or inverse tangent) function returns the "angle whose tangent is" the specified value. The domain for the Arctan is restricted to $-90° < t < 90°$.

Arctan *t*

The *t* indicates a tangent value. (NOTE: You can use your calculator to find Arctan values. Enter a tangent value and activate the **inverse tangent** function. Your calculator will return the angle in the restricted domain.)

Example: Find the angle whose tangent is 5.5.

$$\theta = \textbf{Arctan } 5.5 = 79.7°$$

There are inverse cosecant, inverse secant, and inverse cotangent functions, but they will not be introduced here.

Name: _____ Date: _____

Lesson Seven: Exercises

Complete the following exercises on your own paper.

1. Use your protractor to construct angles of 20°, 30°, 45°, 60°, 90°, 135°, 180°, 225°, 270°, and 315°.

2. Classify the following angles as acute, obtuse, or reflex.

   a) 45°　　　**b)** 105°　　　**c)** 175°　　　**d)** 190°　　　**e)** 88°　　　**f)** 30°

3. Convert the following angles in radians to angles in degrees.

   a) 0.25 radians　　　　**b)** $\pi/4$ radians　　　　**c)** $2\pi/3$ radians

   d) 0.5 radians　　　　　**e)** $3\pi/2$ radians　　　　**f)** 2 radians

4. Convert the following angles in degrees to angles in radians.

   a) 30°　　　**b)** 60°　　　**c)** 45°　　　**d)** 315°　　　**e)** 345°　　　**f)** 190°

5. The radius of a circle is 10 inches. An angle, θ, subtends a distance of 5 inches along the circumference of the circle. What is the angle?

6. The radius of a circle is 4 centimeters. An angle, θ, subtends a distance of 3 centimeters along the circumference of the circle. What is the angle?

7. The radius of a circle is 6 inches. An angle of 1.5 radians subtends an arc of length **s** along the circumference of the circle. What is the length of the arc?

8. The radius of a circle is 25 centimeters. An angle of 0.25 radians subtends an arc of length **s** along the circumference of the circle. What is the length of the arc?

9. Graph **sin θ**, **2sin θ/2**, and **3sin 2θ** on the same axes. Extend the horizontal axis from 360° to 720°. Use your calculator to find the sine values. What are the amplitudes and periods of each of the sinusoidal curves?

10. Graph **sin (θ + 30°)** and **sin (θ - 60°)** on the same axes. Extend the horizontal axis from 360° to 720°. Use your calculator to find the sine values. Note the difference in phase.

11. Graph **cos θ** and **3cos 2θ** on the same axes. Extend the horizontal axis from 360° to 720°. Use your calculator to find the cosine values. What are the amplitudes and periods of the curves?

12. Graph **cos (θ - 45°)** and **cos (θ + 45°)** on the same axes. Extend the horizontal axis from 360° to 720°. Use your calculator to find the cosine values. Note the difference in phase.

13. Graph **2 tan θ** and **tan 2θ** on separate sheets of graph paper. Extend the horizontal axis from 360° to 720°. Use your calculator to find the tangent values. Note the angles where the function goes to plus or minus infinity.

Name: _____ Date: _____

Lesson Seven: Exercises (cont.)

14. Indicate the quadrants (I, II, III, or IV) in which the following trigonometric functions will be negative.

    a) sin   **b)** cos   **c)** tan

In which quadrants will each of them be positive?

15. Use the unit circle in the diagram in this lesson to show that the following relations are true.

    a) $\sin(90° - \theta) = \cos\theta$ **b)** $\cos(90° - \theta) = \sin\theta$

    c) $\sin(180° - \theta) = \sin\theta$ **d)** $\cos(180° - \theta) = -\cos\theta$

    e) $\sin(-\theta) = -\sin\theta$ **f)** $\cos(-\theta) = \cos\theta$

16. Use your calculator and the definition of the given trigonometric function to find the values of the following.

    a) csc 45°   **b)** csc 90°   **c)** sec 30°   **d)** sec 60°   **e)** cot 25°   **f)** cot 80°

17. Start with the identity $\sin^2\theta + \cos^2\theta = 1$.

    a) Divide each term in the equation by $\sin^2\theta$ to develop the new identity,

        $1 + \cot^2\theta = \csc^2\theta$

    b) Use techniques similar to the ones you used in part a) to develop the new identity,

        $\tan^2\theta + 1 = \sec^2\theta$

18. Use your calculator to find the inverse sines of the following.

    a) -1   **b)** 0   **c)** 1   **d)** -0.5774

    e) -0.707   **f)** 0.5   **g)** 0.08749   **h)** 0.866

19. Use your calculator to find the inverse cosines of the following.

    a) 0.5   **b)** 0   **c)** 1   **d)** -0.5

    e) 0.9848   **f)** 0.7071   **g)** -0.866   **h)** -1

20. Use your calculator to find the inverse tangents of the following.

    a) -1   **b)** 0   **c)** 1   **d)** -0.5774

    e) -5.671   **f)** 57.29   **g)** 0.08749   **h)** 1.732

Lesson Eight: Trigonometry

Ezra was working with his friend, Eli, on a Boy Scout project. They had a device that could measure elevation angles and a long tape measure. With these two measuring devices, they were to determine the height of a radio transmitter tower.

"Here's how we will do it," said Ezra. "We will mark off a known distance from the base of the tower. Then, at that distance, we will measure the angle from horizontal to the top of the tower. Finally, we will use trigonometry to calculate the height of the tower."

RIGHT-TRIANGLE TRIGONOMETRY

Ezra and Eli were using some of the most common applications of angles, sines, cosines, and tangents. They were solving a problem that involved a **right triangle**. A right triangle is a three-sided figure in which two of the sides are perpendicular. A typical right triangle is shown below. The lengths of the two short sides are **a** and **b**, and the length of the long side, the **hypotenuse**, is labeled **c**. The angle opposite side **a** is α, and the angle opposite side **b** is β. The angle opposite the hypotenuse is a 90° or right angle.

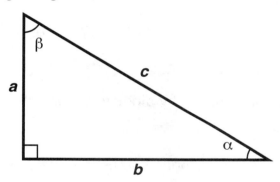

Problems in right-triangle trigonometry involve right triangles in which some quantities, either angles or side lengths, are known, and others are to be calculated. There are five quantities altogether: **a**, **b**, **c**, α, and β. If an angle and a side or two sides are known, then the other three values can be determined. There are five equations that can be used.

The Pythagorean Theorem

$$c^2 = a^2 + b^2$$

The sum of the angles in a triangle

The sum of the angles in a triangle is 180°. Therefore, **$a + b + 90° = 180°$** or **$a + b = 90$**.

Lesson Eight: Trigonometry (cont.)

The sine, cosine, and tangent functions

In a right triangle, like the one on the previous page, the trig functions can be defined as shown below.

$$\sin \alpha = \frac{\text{side opposite}}{\text{hypotenuse}} = \frac{a}{c} \qquad\qquad \sin \beta = \frac{\text{side opposite}}{\text{hypotenuse}} = \frac{b}{c}$$

$$\cos \alpha = \frac{\text{side adjacent}}{\text{hypotenuse}} = \frac{b}{c} \qquad\qquad \cos \beta = \frac{\text{side adjacent}}{\text{hypotenuse}} = \frac{a}{c}$$

$$\tan \alpha = \frac{\text{side opposite}}{\text{side adjacent}} = \frac{a}{b} \qquad\qquad \tan \beta = \frac{\text{side opposite}}{\text{side adjacent}} = \frac{b}{a}$$

The following examples show how these equations can be manipulated to solve triangle problems.

Examples:

1) Side a of the triangle is 4 units long, and angle β is 30°. Find sides b and c and angle α.

$$\alpha = 90° - \beta = 90° - 30° = 60°$$

$$\sin \alpha = a/c \qquad\qquad c = a/\sin \alpha = 4/\sin 60°$$
$$= 4/0.866 = 4.62 \text{ units}$$

$$\cos \alpha = b/c \qquad\qquad b = c \cos \alpha = 4.62 \cos 60°$$
$$= 4.62 \times 0.5 = 2.31 \text{ units}$$

2) Side a of the triangle is 3 cm long, and side b is 4 cm long. Find side c and angles α and β.

$$\tan \alpha = a/b = \tfrac{3}{4} = 0.75$$

$$\alpha = \text{Arctan } 0.75 = 36.87°$$

$$\beta = 90° - \alpha = 90° - 36.87° = 53.13°$$

$$c^2 = a^2 + b^2 \qquad\qquad c = \sqrt{a^2 + b^2}$$

$$= \sqrt{3^2 + 4^2} = \sqrt{25}$$

$$= 5 \text{ cm}$$

Lesson Eight: Trigonometry (cont.)

3) Side **a** of the triangle is 5 ft. long, and the hypotenuse (**c**) is 13 ft. long. Find side **b** and angles α and β.

$$\sin \alpha = 5/13 = 0.3846$$

$$\alpha = \text{Arcsin } 0.3846 = 22.6°$$

$$\cos \alpha = b/13$$

$$b = 13 \cos 22.6° = 12 \text{ ft.}$$

$$\beta = 90° - \alpha = 90° - 22.6° = 67.4°$$

TRIGONOMETRIC FORMULAS

In calculus, trigonometric forms are often encountered. Many of them can be simplified by the application of some simple trigonometric formulas. The most common of these formulas are listed below.

Sum and Difference of Angles Formulas

$$\sin (\alpha + \beta) = \sin \alpha \cos \beta + \cos \alpha \sin \beta$$

$$\sin (\alpha - \beta) = \sin \alpha \cos \beta - \cos \alpha \sin \beta$$

$$\cos (\alpha + \beta) = \cos \alpha \cos \beta - \sin \alpha \sin \beta$$

$$\cos (\alpha - \beta) = \cos \alpha \cos \beta + \sin \alpha \sin \beta$$

$$\tan (\alpha + \beta) = \frac{\tan \alpha + \tan \beta}{1 - \tan \alpha \tan \beta}$$

$$\tan (\alpha - \beta) = \frac{\tan \alpha - \tan \beta}{1 + \tan \alpha \tan \beta}$$

These formulas can be used to express sums or differences of angles in terms of trigonometric functions of the angles themselves. They can take many forms.

Examples:

1) Find **cos(θ + 90°)**

$$\cos(\theta + 90°) = \cos \theta \cos 90° - \sin \theta \sin 90°$$
$$= \cos \theta (0) - \sin \theta (1)$$
$$= -\sin \theta$$

Lesson Eight: Trigonometry (cont.)

2) Find **tan(Arctan 3 + Arctan 4)**

$$\tan(\text{Arctan } 3 + \text{Arctan } 4) = \frac{\tan(\text{Arctan } 3) + \tan(\text{Arctan } 4)}{1 - \tan(\text{Arctan } 3)\tan(\text{Arctan } 4)}$$

$$= \frac{3 + 4}{1 - 3(4)} = -\tfrac{7}{11}$$

$$= -\tfrac{7}{11}$$

3) Find **sin 3θ**

$$
\begin{aligned}
\sin 3\theta = \sin(2\theta + \theta) &= \sin 2\theta \cos \theta + \cos 2\theta \sin \theta \\
&= (\sin \theta \cos \theta + \cos \theta \sin \theta)\cos \theta + (\cos \theta \cos \theta - \sin \theta \sin \theta)\sin \theta \\
&= 2 \sin \theta \cos \theta \cos \theta + (\cos^2 \theta - \sin^2 \theta)\sin \theta \\
&= 2 \sin \theta \cos^2 \theta + \cos^2 \theta \sin \theta - \sin^3 \theta \\
&= 3 \sin \theta \cos^2 \theta - \sin^3 \theta \\
&= 3 \sin \theta(1 - \sin^2 \theta) - \sin^3 \theta \\
&= 3 \sin \theta - 4 \sin^3 \theta
\end{aligned}
$$

Double Angle Formulas

If α and β are both the same angle in the sum of angles formulas above, the following **double angle formulas** result.

$$\sin 2\theta = 2 \sin \theta \cos \theta$$

$$\cos 2\theta = \cos^2 \theta - \sin^2 \theta = 1 - 2 \sin^2 \theta = 2 \cos^2 \theta - 1$$

$$\tan 2\theta = \frac{2 \tan \theta}{1 - \tan^2 \theta}$$

Like the sum and difference formulas, the double angle formulas can be used to compute values or change the form of existing trig equations.

Example:

1) Find **cos 4θ**

$$
\begin{aligned}
\cos 4\theta &= 2 \cos^2 2\theta - 1 \\
&= 2(2 \cos^2 \theta - 1)^2 - 1 \\
&= 2(4 \cos^4 \theta - 4 \cos^2 \theta + 1) - 1 \\
&= 8 \cos^4 \theta - 8 \cos^2 \theta + 1
\end{aligned}
$$

Lesson Eight: Trigonometry (cont.)

2) If θ is an acute angle in a right triangle and $\sin \theta = x$, show that $\sin 2\theta = (2)1 - x^2$.

If $\sin \theta = x$, then $\cos \theta = 1 - x^2$.

$\sin 2\theta = 2 \sin \theta \cos \theta = (2)1 - x^2$

Half Angle Formulas

The half angle formulas can be developed from the double angle formulas above (if you are willing to do a little manipulation). We will simply write them below.

$$\sin \frac{\theta}{2} = \sqrt{\frac{1 - \cos \theta}{2}}$$

$$\cos \frac{\theta}{2} = \sqrt{\frac{1 + \cos \theta}{2}}$$

$$\tan \frac{\theta}{2} = \frac{1 - \cos \theta}{\sin \theta} = \frac{\sin \theta}{1 + \cos \theta}$$

These formulas can also be used to simplify trigonometric expressions.

Example:

Show that $2 \cos^2 \frac{\theta}{2} \tan \frac{\theta}{2} = \sin \theta$

$$2 \cos^2 \frac{\theta}{2} \tan \frac{\theta}{2} = 2 \frac{1 + \cos \theta}{2} \quad \frac{\sin \theta}{1 + \cos \theta}$$

$$= \sin \theta$$

Name: _____ Date: _____

Lesson Eight: Exercises

Complete the following exercises on your own paper.

1. The following problems refer to the right triangle introduced in this lesson.

a) Side **a** of a right triangle is 120 inches long and the hypotenuse (**c**) is 130 inches long. Find side **b** and the angles α and β.

b) Side **a** of a right triangle is 6 ft. long and angle α is 36.87°. Find sides **b** and **c** and the angle β.

c) Side **b** of a right triangle is 10 cm long and angle α is 30°. Find sides **a** and **c** and the angle β.

d) Side **a** of a right triangle is 8 cm long and side **b** is 5 cm long. Find side **c** and the angles α and β.

e) Side **a** of a right triangle is 9 meters long and the hypotenuse (**c**) is 18 meters long. Find side **b** and the angles α and β.

f) Side **b** of a right triangle is 14 cm long and angle β is 50°. Find sides **a** and **c** and the angle α.

g) Side **a** of a right triangle is 20 ft. long and angle β is 70°. Find sides **b** and **c** and the angle α.

h) Side **a** of a right triangle is 7 inches long and side **b** is 9 inches long. Find side **c** and the angles α and β.

2. Use the sum and difference of angles formulas to evaluate the following expressions.

a) $\cos 30° \cos 20° - \sin 30° \sin 20°$

b) $\sin 30° \cos 20° + \sin 20° \cos 30°$

c) $\dfrac{\tan 20° - \tan 40°}{1 + \tan 20° \tan 40°}$

d) $\cos 30° \sin 20° - \sin 30° \cos 20°$

3. Use the sum and difference formulas to show that the following "reduction formulas" are true.

a) $\sin (180° - \theta) = \sin \theta$

b) $\sin (180° + \theta) = -\sin \theta$

c) $\cos (180° - \theta) = -\cos \theta$

d) $\cos (180° + \theta) = -\cos \theta$

e) $\tan (180° - \theta) = -\tan \theta$

f) $\tan (180° + \theta) = \tan \theta$

Name: _____ Date: _____

Lesson Eight: Exercises (cont.)

g) $\sin(90° - \theta) = \cos\theta$ **h)** $\sin(90° + \theta) = \cos\theta$

i) $\cos(90° - \theta) = \sin\theta$ **j)** $\cos(90° + \theta) = -\sin\theta$

k) $\tan(90° - \theta) = \cot\theta$ **l)** $\tan(90° + \theta) = -\cot\theta$

4. Use the sum and difference of angles formulas to verify the following identities. Work with the left-hand side of the equation to make it identical to the right-hand side.

a) $\sin 2\theta = 2\sin\theta\cos\theta$ **b)** $\cos 2\theta = 2\cos^2\theta - 1$

c) $\cos 3\theta = 4\cos^3\theta - 3\cos\theta$ **d)** $\tan 3\theta = \dfrac{3\tan\theta - \tan^3\theta}{1 - 3\tan^2\theta}$

e) $\dfrac{\sin 2\theta}{\tan\theta} = 2\cos^2\theta$ **f)** $\sin(\alpha + \beta) - \sin(\alpha - \beta) = 2\cos\alpha\sin\beta$

g) $\cos(\alpha + \beta) + \cos(\alpha - \beta) = 2\cos\alpha\cos\beta$

h) $\dfrac{\sin(\alpha + \beta)}{\sin(\alpha - \beta)} = \dfrac{\tan\alpha + \tan\beta}{\tan\alpha - \tan\beta}$

5. If $\tan\alpha = \frac{3}{4}$ and $0° < \alpha < 90°$, find the following, using the double angle formulas.

a) $\tan 2\alpha$ **b)** $\sin 2\alpha$ **c)** $\cos 2\alpha$

6. Use the known values, **$\sin 90° = 1$** and **$\cos 90° = 0$**, and the half angle formulas to find the following.

a) $\sin 45°$ **b)** $\cos 45°$

7. Use the double angle formulas to verify the following identities. Work with the left-hand side of the equation to make it identical to the right-hand side. (NOTE: In some of the following problems, you may have to factor a trig expression. Example: **$\sin^2\theta - \cos^2\theta = (\sin\theta + \cos\theta)(\sin\theta - \cos\theta)$**.)

a) $\cos^4\theta - \sin^4\theta = \cos 2\theta$ **b)** $\dfrac{\sin 2\theta}{1 + \cos 2\theta} = \tan\theta$

c) $\sin 2\alpha = 2\tan\alpha\cos^2\alpha$ **d)** $(\sin\theta + \cos\theta)^2 = 1 + \sin 2\theta$

e) $\frac{1}{2}\sin 2\beta = \dfrac{\tan\beta}{1 + \tan^2\beta}$ **f)** $\dfrac{\sin\theta + \sin 2\theta}{1 + \cos\theta + \cos 2\theta} = \tan\theta$

Name: _____ Date: _____

Lesson Eight: Exercises (cont.)

g) $\tan 2\beta = \dfrac{2}{\cot \beta - \tan \beta}$

h) $\sin 4\alpha = 8 \sin \alpha \cos^3 \alpha - 4 \sin \alpha \cos \alpha$

8. Use the half angle formulas to verify the following identities. Work with the left-hand side of the equation to make it equal to the right-hand side.

a) $\cos^2 \dfrac{\theta}{2} = \dfrac{\tan \theta + \sin \theta}{2 \tan \theta}$

b) $\dfrac{2 \tan \dfrac{\theta}{2}}{1 + \tan^2 \dfrac{\theta}{2}} = \sin \theta$

c) $\cos \theta = \dfrac{1 - \tan^2 \dfrac{\theta}{2}}{1 + \tan^2 \dfrac{\theta}{2}}$

d) $\dfrac{2}{\tan \dfrac{\alpha}{2} + \cot \dfrac{\alpha}{2}} = \sin \alpha$

e) $\sin^4 \dfrac{\alpha}{2} = \frac{1}{4} - \frac{1}{2} \cos \alpha + \frac{1}{4} \cos^2 \alpha$

f) $\sec^2 \dfrac{x}{2} = \dfrac{2}{1 + \cos x}$

9. Use the half angle formulas to develop the following "power formulas."

a) $\sin^2 \theta = \dfrac{1 - \cos 2\theta}{2}$

b) $\cos^2 \theta = \dfrac{1 + \cos 2\theta}{2}$

c) $\tan^2 \theta = \dfrac{1 - \cos 2\theta}{1 + \cos 2\theta}$

Lesson Nine: Graphing Functions

Marcus was doing his math homework and had run into a problem. The homework was about graphing functions, and he had run into a function that he could not graph. In fact, even though the function was a polynomial, he could not even get started. Fortunately, Marcus's father was an engineer and was able to help.

"You can plot a graph from a table of values," he said, "but sometimes that is hard to do. You can make things easier if you look for special properties of the function that you are trying to graph."

"For example, look at your function," he continued. "If you set $y = 0$ and solve for the roots of the equation, you can find the places where the graph crosses the x-axis. Also, a simple test you can perform will show you that your function is symmetric with respect to the y-axis. This means that the part of your graph to the left of the y-axis is a mirror image of the part to the right of the y-axis."

Marcus listened intently as his father explained several other properties of functions and graphs. After the conversation, he was able to quickly complete his graphing assignment.

GRAPHING A FUNCTION

In Lesson Two you learned how to graph and analyze a linear function, in Lesson Four you were introduced to graphs of quadratic functions, and in Lessons Six and Seven you saw graphs of exponential, logarithmic, and trigonometric functions. As you probably noticed, each type of graph has its own special features. Some of these features can be used to help you graph a particular function.

The most straightforward way to produce a graph of a function is to generate a table of values and then plot the points from this table on graph paper. The figure below shows a table of values for the function $y = f(x) = x^3 - 6x^2 + 11x - 6$.

x	y
0	-6
0.5	-1.875
1	0
1.5	0.375
2	0
2.5	-0.375
3	0
3.5	1.875
4	6

Graph A:

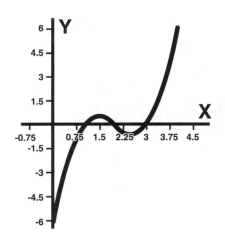

This technique allowed an approximation of the graph to be drawn. If a very detailed plot was desired, more points would have to be added to the table. Some things about the graph are obvious, however. One is that the graph crosses the x-axis at three points. Therefore, the function must have three real roots.

Lesson Nine: Graphing Functions (cont.)

Real Roots of Functions

The points where a function crosses the x-axis are the **real roots** of the function. In many cases, they can be found quickly by setting the function to zero and then solving for the values of x. There is, of course, no guarantee that a function has real roots. Two theorems from algebra, however, are sometimes useful to remember when the function is a polynomial.

Fundamental Theorem of Algebra

If $f(x)$ is a polynomial of degree ≥ 1, then $f(x) = 0$ has at least one real or complex root.

N-Roots Theorem

If $f(x)$ is a polynomial of degree ≥ 1, then $f(x)$ has a number of (real or complex) roots equal to the degree of the function. Some of the roots may be multiple roots (i.e. more than one root with the same value).

These theorems tell you to start looking for a certain number of roots when you are dealing with a polynomial. You may not find them (they may all be complex), but it is a good place to start. The following comments will help you visualize the behavior of a polynomial curve at a root.

1) If there is a single root at $x = a$, the curve will cross the x-axis at $x = a$. There will be no change in the curvature of the function.

2) If there is a double root at $x = a$ (two roots, each with the value $x = a$), the function will touch the x-axis at $x = a$, but it will then turn around and go back in the direction that it came from. It will <u>not</u> cross the x-axis. The function is said to have a **relative maximum** or a **relative minimum** point at $x = a$.

3) If there is a triple root at $x = a$ (three roots, each with the value $x = a$), the function will cross the x-axis at $x = a$, but it will change the nature of its slope when it crosses.

Higher orders of multiple roots will have many of the same properties. In general, the graph will not cross the x-axis at even multiple roots and will cross it at odd ones. The graphs on the next page show the behavior of three polynomials that have roots at $x = 2$. The first one, $y = x^2 - 4$, has a single root; the second one, $y = x^2 - 4x + 4$, has a double root; and the third one, $y = x^3 - 6x^2 + 12x - 8$, has a triple root.

Lesson Nine: Graphing Functions (cont.)

Graph B:

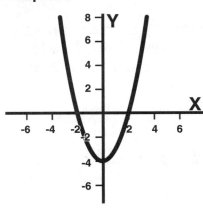

$y = x^2 - 4$

Graph C:

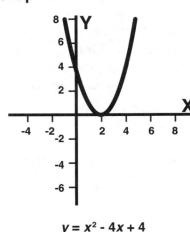

$y = x^2 - 4x + 4$

Graph D:

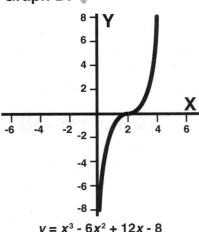

$y = x^3 - 6x^2 + 12x - 8$

Symmetry

Some functions are symmetric about the y-axis or the origin. If a function is symmetric about the y-axis, the part of your graph to the left of the y-axis is a mirror image of the part to the right of the y-axis. If a function is symmetric with respect to the origin, half of the graph looks like it has been rotated 180° with respect to the other half. The figures below show a function that is symmetric about the y-axis, $y = x^2$, and another function that is symmetric about the origin, $y = x^3$.

Graph E:

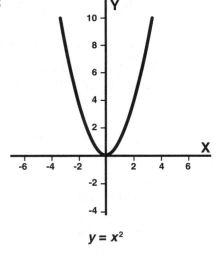

$y = x^2$

Graph F:

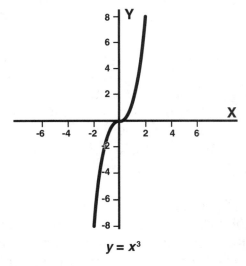

$y = x^3$

The following tests can determine whether or not a function is symmetric.

If $f(x) = f(-x)$, the function is symmetric with respect to the y-axis.

If $f(-x) = -f(x)$, the function is symmetric with respect to the origin.

Lesson Nine: Graphing Functions (cont.)

Scaling

Multiplying an existing function by a constant can change the vertical scale of the function. If the constant is greater than 1, then the new function will appear to be "stretched out" in the vertical dimension, and if the constant is less than 1, then the function will appear to be "squashed" in the vertical dimension. Multiplying by 1, of course, leaves the function unchanged, but multiplying by -1 causes the function to be its mirror image on the other side of the x-axis. The graph below shows plots of $y = x^2$, $y = -x^2$, and $y = 6x^2$.

Graph G:

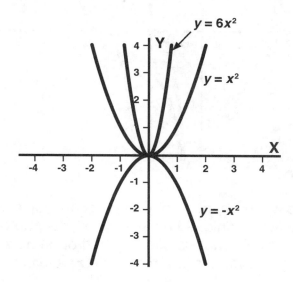

Translating

Adding a constant to a function can shift the function graph upward or downward in the vertical direction.

$y = f(x) + a$ is $y = f(x)$ shifted upward by a units.

$y = f(x) - a$ is $y = f(x)$ shifted downward by a units.

Adding a constant to the variable can shift the graph of the function to the left or to the right.

$y = f(x + a)$ is $y = f(x)$ shifted to the right by a units.

$y = f(x - a)$ is $y = f(x)$ shifted to the left by a units.

Lesson Nine: Graphing Functions (cont.)

The graph below shows the plots of $y = x^3$, $y = x^3 - 3$, and $y = (x - 3)^3$.

Graph H:

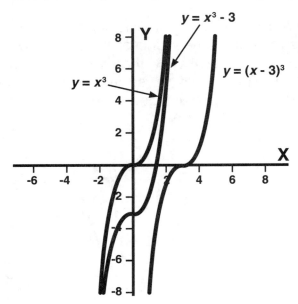

Absolute Value Functions

Functions that can be written in the form $y = |f(x)|$ are sometimes called **absolute value functions**. This type of function is unique because all of the graph is on or above the x-axis. None of the graph can extend below the x-axis. A graph of an absolute value function can be easily obtained by pretending that you are graphing $y = f(x)$ and then reflecting the portion of the graph that extends below the x-axis about the x-axis. The graph of $y = |x^2 - 4|$ in the diagram below shows how this can be done.

Graph I:

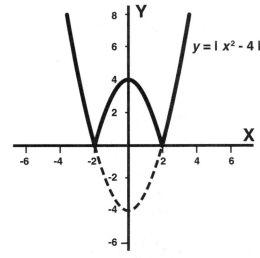

The portions of the graph to the extreme left and extreme right and the dotted line portion make up the graph of $y = x^2 - 4$. The dotted line portion is not, however, part of the graph of $y = |x^2 - 4|$. When the dotted line portion (the part below the x-axis) is reflected about the x-axis, the center, solid-line portion above the x-axis becomes a part of the graph of $y = |x^2 - 4|$.

Lesson Nine: Graphing Functions (cont.)

DESCRIPTIVE PROPERTIES OF FUNCTION GRAPHS

Slopes

The **slope** of a linear function is a constant, but the slopes of other curves vary from point to point. The slope of a function that is not linear must be expressed at a given point. It is usually defined as the slope of a line tangent to the function at the point in question. The graph below shows a curve, a tangent line, and the slope of the tangent line.

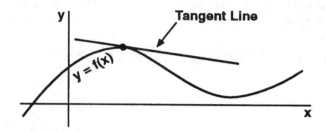

A property that is related to the slope is the **concavity** of a function at different points. Portions of the graph of a function where the slope increases as x increases are said to be **concave upward**. Portions of the graph where the slope decreases as x increases are **concave downward**. This concavity is usually not something that you can easily see before you graph a function, but it is often apparent from the graph.

Points on the graph of a function where the graph changes from concave upward to concave downward, or from concave downward to concave upward, are called **inflection points**. A good example of an inflection point is at $x = 0$ on the graph of $y = x^3$.

A point on the graph of a function where the graph rises to a high point and then descends again is called a **relative maximum** (or **local maximum**) point. A point where the graph descends to a low point and then rises again is called a **relative minimum** (or **local minimum**) point. The figure below shows a graph of $y = x^3 + 2x^2 + x + 1$. It has a relative maximum at $x = -1$ and a relative minimum at $x = -\frac{1}{3}$.

Graph J:

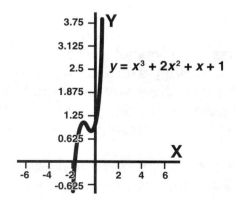

If a maximum point is the highest value in the entire range of the function, it is an **absolute maximum**. If a minimum point is the lowest value in the entire range of the function, it is an **absolute minimum**.

Lesson Nine: Graphing Functions (cont.)

Asymptotes

In Lesson Six you saw that the graph of $y = 2^x$ approached the x-axis as x became large and negative. The x-axis in this case was an asymptote.

In general, an **asymptote** is a straight line that the graph of a function gets closer and closer to as a point moves along the graph. The line is said to be an asymptote of the function, and the graph of the function is said to approach the line asymptotically. The graph of a function can have more than one asymptote. Asymptotes can be horizontal, vertical, or lines with finite positive or negative slopes. A function will approach a horizontal asymptote as x goes to infinity in the positive or negative direction. It will approach a vertical asymptote as x gets closer and closer to some finite value.

Two good examples of functions with asymptotes are $y = 1/x$ and $y = 1/x^2$.

Graph K: **Graph L:**

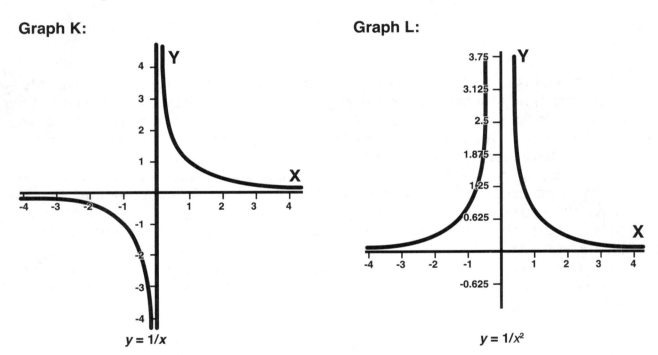

$y = 1/x$ $y = 1/x^2$

The function $y = 1/x$ has two asymptotes, the y-axis and the x-axis. The $y = 1/x^2$ function also has two asymptotes, the positive y-axis and the x-axis.

A class of functions that often have vertical asymptotes are rational functions. A **rational function** contains a ratio of polynomials, one in its numerator and another in its denominator. The following rule allows you to quickly determine the vertical asymptotes of a rational function.

The graph of a rational function will have a vertical asymptote at each point where the denominator is 0 and the numerator is not 0.

Lesson Nine: Graphing Functions (cont.)

The graphs of the rational functions

$$y = \frac{5}{x-3} \quad \text{and} \quad y = \frac{x+5}{x^2+x-2} = \frac{x+5}{(x-1)(x+2)}$$

are shown below.

Graph M: **Graph N:**

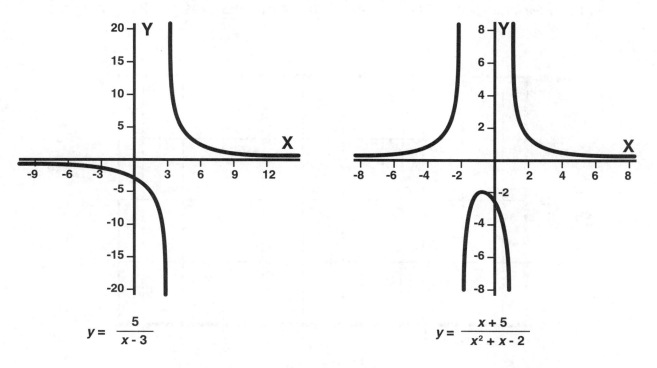

$$y = \frac{5}{x-3} \qquad\qquad y = \frac{x+5}{x^2+x-2}$$

The first function has an asymptote at $x = 3$, and the second one has two vertical asymptotes, one at $x = -2$ and another at $x = 1$.

Lesson Nine: Graphing Functions (cont.)

LOG-LINEAR AND LOG-LOG GRAPHS

All of the graphs we have looked at so far have been plotted on linear axes. A **linear axis** is one that has equally spaced divisions along the axis line. It is possible, however, to have an axis whose divisions are not equally spaced. One type of coordinate axis, called a **log axis**, has divisions that are spaced in such a way that each division is a multiple of the previous one. Usually the divisions are powers of 2, 10, or **e**, or some other number that is used as a logarithmic base.

A popular type of graph is one that has a log axis on the vertical and a linear horizontal axis. It is called a **log-linear graph**. The diagram below shows the axes of a log-linear graph.

Graph O:

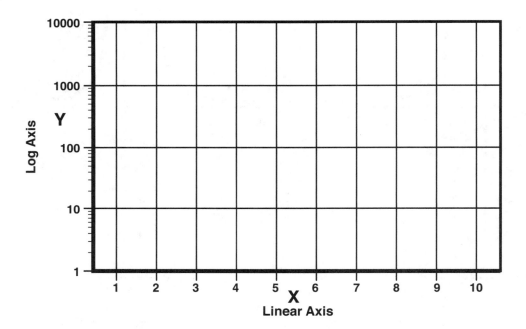

Plotting a function on a log-linear set of coordinate axes is equivalent to plotting (on ordinary linear coordinate axes) the logarithm (to some base) of the vertical values versus the horizontal values. It is interesting because an exponential equation will show up as a straight line on a log-linear graph. To see why, consider the derivation below.

$$y = ab^x \qquad (\textbf{\textit{a}} \text{ and } \textbf{\textit{b}} \text{ are real number constants})$$

$$\log y = \log (ab^x)$$

$$= \log b^x + \log a$$

$$= x \log b + \log a$$

Lesson Nine: Graphing Functions (cont.)

This equation would produce a straight line (with **slope = log *b*** and **vertical intercept = log *a*)** if **log *y*** were plotted on the vertical axis versus **x** on the horixontal one. As an example, the exponential equation, **y = 4 · 2^x**, is plotted on the log-linear axes that follow.

Graph P:

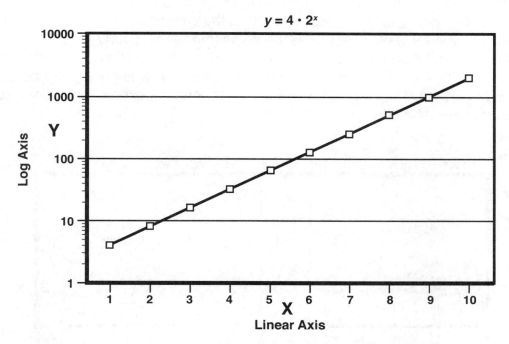

A type of graph that has log axes on both the vertical and horizontal is called a **log-log graph**. Plotting **y** versus **x** values on a log-log graph is equivalent to plotting **log *y*** versus **log *x*** values on an ordinary linear graph. Functions of the form, **y = ax^b** (where **a** and **b** are real number constants), appear as straight lines on log-log graphs. The following derivation shows why.

$$y = ax^b$$

$$\log y = \log (ax^b)$$

$$\log y = \log x^b + \log a$$

$$\log y = b \log x + \log a$$

This equation would be a straight line if **log *y*** were plotted versus **log *x*** on linear axes. It would also be a straight line if **y** were plotted versus **x** on log-log axes.

Lesson Nine: Graphing Functions (cont.)

POLAR GRAPHS

Some functions are more easily expressed in terms of polar coordinates than in terms of *x-y* coordinates. **Polar coordinates** are ordered pairs of numbers like the *x* and *y* values used in rectangular coordinates. In the polar system, however, the numbers are called *r* and θ, and the coordinates of a point are (*r*, θ). The *r* value specifies the distance to a point from the origin of the coordinate system, and the θ value specifies the angle (measured counterclockwise) between the **positive polar axis** and a line from the origin to the point. The positive polar axis is in the same direction as the positive *x*-axis in an *x-y* coordinate system. The angle, θ, can be expressed in either degrees or radians. The diagram below shows four points expressed in polar coordinates. Note that the axes are labeled 0°, 90°, 180°, and 270°.

Graph Q:

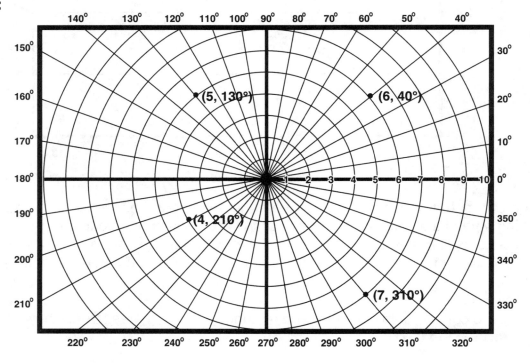

A function, in polar form, is usually expressed as *r* = *f*(θ). The following functions are some typical examples.

$$r = 2 \cos \theta$$

$$r = 3 (1 + \sin \theta)$$

$$r = \sin 2\theta$$

Lesson Nine: Graphing Functions (cont.)

Polar functions, such as these, can be plotted on special polar graph paper. Polar paper has values of r indicated by concentric circles and values of θ specified by straight lines that radiate outward from the origin. The figures below show $r = 1 + \sin \theta$ and $r = \sin 2\theta$ plotted on polar graph paper.

Graph R: **Graph S:**

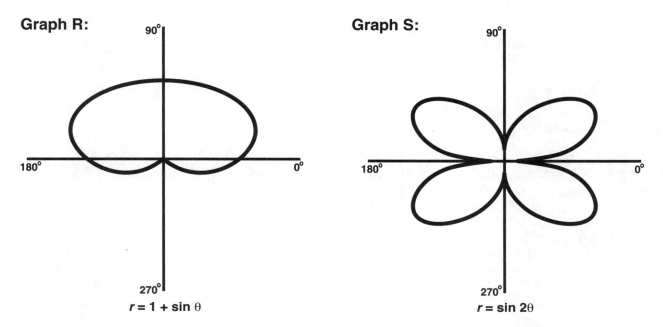

$r = 1 + \sin \theta$ $r = \sin 2\theta$

A polar graph may be constructed in much the same way as a graph with rectangular coordinates is produced. First create a table of r, θ coordinate pairs, and then plot the individual points on the graph. After you have plotted several polar graphs, you will begin to notice some symmetries that make the task easier.

Conversion Between Polar and Rectangular Coordinates

It is easy to convert between polar and rectangular coordinates. To see how, consider the diagram below.

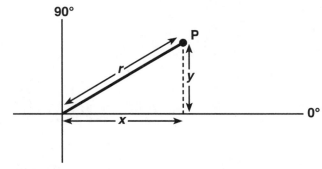

The point **P** has polar coordinates (r, θ) and rectangular coordinates (x, y). The point **P**, the origin, and the point where a perpendicular from **P** intersects the x-axis form a right triangle whose hypotenuse is r. The conversion from rectangular coordinates to polar ones is straightforward.

Lesson Nine: Graphing Functions (cont.)

From the Pythagorean Theorem,

$$r^2 = x^2 + y^2$$

$$r = \sqrt{x^2 + y^2}$$

From the definition of the tangent,

$$\tan \theta = \frac{y}{x}$$

$$\theta = \text{Arctan}\left(\frac{y}{x}\right)$$

The conversion from polar to rectangular coordinates can be obtained from the definitions of the sine and cosine.

$$\sin \theta = \frac{y}{r}$$

$$y = r \sin \theta$$

$$\cos \theta = \frac{x}{r}$$

$$x = r \cos \theta$$

The above conversions emphasize that the 0° axis is in the same direction as the positive x-axis, the 90° axis is in the same direction as the +y-axis, the 180° axis is directed in the -x direction, and the 270° axis is in the -y direction. The diagram on page 96 is divided into four quadrants. The signs of the (x, y) coordinates in each of these quadrants are summarized below.

Quadrant	x	y
I	+	+
II	-	+
III	-	-
IV	+	-

Name: _____ Date: _____

Lesson Nine: Exercises

Complete the following exercises on your own paper.

1. The following functions have one or more real roots. Find the roots and graph the functions.

    a) $y = x^2 - 3x + 2$ **b)** $y = x^2 + x - 2$

    c) $y = x^3 - 2x^2 - x + 2$ **d)** $y = x^3 - 5x^2 - 2x + 24$

    e) $y = (x - 3)(x - 6)(x - 10)$ **f)** $y = (x + 2)(x + 1)(x - 3)(x - 4)$

2. The following functions have double roots. Find the roots and graph the functions.

    a) $y = x^2 - 2x + 1$ **b)** $y = (x - 5)^2$ **c)** $y = (x + 1)(x - 3)^2$

3. The following functions have triple roots. Find the triple roots and graph the functions.

    a) $y = x^3 + 6x^2 + 12x + 8$ **b)** $y = (x - 4)^3$ **c)** $y = (x - 1)^3 (x - 5)$

4. Plot the function $y = x^3$ and the scaled versions of it, $y = 2x^3$ and $y = -2x^3$, on the same axes.

5. Which of the following functions are symmetric with respect to the y-axis, symmetric with respect to the origin, or not symmetric with respect to either the y-axis or the origin? Do not plot the functions.

    a) $y = x^5$ **b)** $y = x^4$ **c)** $y = 4x^3 - 7$

    d) $y = x^2 - 2x + 1$ **e)** $y = 64x^6$ **f)** $y = -2x^7$

    g) $y = (x - 3)(x + 4)$ **h)** $y = (x + 9)^3$ **i)** $y = x$

6. Plot the following functions and indicate if they are symmetric with respect to the y-axis or the origin.

    a) $y = x^4$ **b)** $y = x^5$ **c)** $y = 4x^2$ **d)** $y = -8x^3$

7. Plot the following familiar, but translated functions.

    a) $y = x^3 + 3$ **b)** $y = x^3 - 2$ **c)** $y = (x + 2)^3$

    d) $y = (x + 3)^2$ **e)** $y = (x - 2)^2 - 2$ **f)** $y = (x + 1)^3 + 3$

Name: _____ Date: _____

Lesson Nine: Exercises (cont.)

8. Plot the following absolute value functions.

    a) $y = | x^2 - 8 |$ **b)** $y = | x^3 |$ **c)** $y = | x^3 - 1 |$

    d) $y = | x + 2 |$ **e)** $y = | (x + 2)^2 - 2 |$ **f)** $y = | (x - 1)^2 - 3 |$

9. Which regions of the following graphs are concave upward and which are concave downward?

    a) 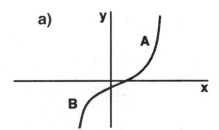   **b)**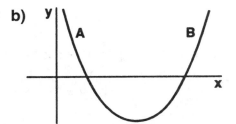

    c) 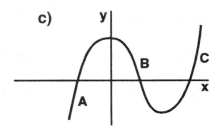   **d)**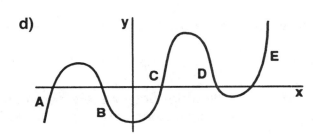

10. Which of the following points are relative maximum points, relative minimum points, or inflection points?

    a) 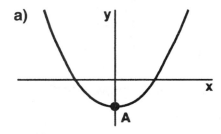   **b)**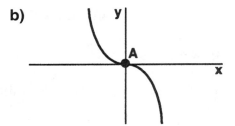

    c) 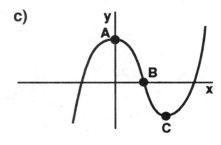   **d)**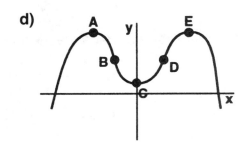

Name: _____ Date: _____

Lesson Nine: Exercises (cont.)

11. Plot the following curves and identify any vertical asymptotes.

  a) $y = \dfrac{4}{x^2}$

  b) $y = 4 - \frac{1}{2}x$

  c) $y = \dfrac{1}{x - 31}$

  d) $y = \dfrac{1}{x - 2} + 2$

  e) $y = \dfrac{x}{x^2 - 7x + 12}$

  f) $y = \dfrac{x + 3}{(x - 4)(x + 1)}$

  g) $y = \dfrac{x + 6}{x^2 + 5x - 6}$

  h) $y = \dfrac{x - 2}{x^2 - 4}$

  i) $y = \dfrac{x + 2}{x^2 + 4x + 4}$

12. Plot the exponential function below (for the domain $0 \le x \le 4$) on ordinary linear graph paper. Then plot it again (for the domain $1 \le x \le 9$) on log-linear paper.

  $y = 2^x$

13. Plot the exponential function below (for the domain $0 \le x \le 3$) on ordinary linear graph paper. Then plot it again (for the domain $1 \le x \le 6$) on log-linear paper.

  $y = 4 \cdot 2^{2x}$

14. Plot the function below on ordinary linear graph paper (for the domain $0 \le x \le 4$). Then plot it again (for the domain $1 \le x \le 8$) on log-log paper.

  $y = 3x^3$

15. Plot the following functions on polar graph paper.

  a) $r = 1 + 2\sin\theta$

  b) $r = \cos 2\theta$

  c) $r = 3 + 3\cos\theta$

  d) $r = 3\cos 3\theta$

  e) $r = \dfrac{2}{\cos\theta}$

  f) $r = \dfrac{1}{1 - \sin\theta}$

16. Convert the following polar coordinates to x-y coordinates.

  a) $(5, 30°)$

  b) $(4, 130°)$

  c) $(6, 200°)$

  d) $(4, 330°)$

  e) $(2, 60°)$

  f) $(5, 45°)$

  g) $(5, 90°)$

  h) $(3, 0°)$

17. Convert the following x-y coordinates to polar coordinates.

  a) $(4, 3)$

  b) $(3, 6)$

  c) $(4, 0)$

  d) $(5, 5)$

  e) $(-3, 1)$

  f) $(-12, -5)$

  g) $(4, -2)$

  h) $(0, 3)$

Lesson Ten: Sequences and Series

Quarette was leaving a two-hour set of achievement and aptitude tests that were administered by her school. Although she was exhausted, she felt that she had done really well. The only thing that had bothered her was a short section of one test that had shown a list of numbers and then asked for the next number in what was called a sequence. Quarette was puzzled and asked her best friend, Claudine, about sequences.

"Don't worry," Claudine replied. "Sequences are just sets of elements that are ordered in certain ways. You will learn all about them next year in pre-calculus."

SEQUENCES

In much of the mathematics that you have studied so far, you have been concerned with the properties of real numbers and various functions of real numbers. In some applications, however, ordered sets of numbers—real, natural, or integer—are of interest. In this section, we will look at some ordered sets called sequences.

A **sequence** is just an ordered set of numbers. The numbers in a sequence are often called **terms**. The set of numbers that makes up a sequence can be finite or infinite. An example of an infinite sequence could be the set of positive integers $\{1, 2, 3, 4, 5, \ldots\}$. An example of a finite sequence could be the set $\{1, 2, 4, 8, 16\}$.

The ordering of a sequence must be specified in some way. In some cases, it is easiest just to list the terms or to define each term in a way that relates it to the preceding term or to several preceding terms. In other cases, it is easier to construct a formula that specifies the value of each term, usually as some general or nth term. Some sequences and their representations are shown below.

{3, 12, 19, 27, 39}

This is a finite sequence whose terms are simply listed.

{2, 4, 6, 8, 10, 12, …}

This is the infinite sequence of the even, non-negative integers.

$t_n = 3n - 1$

This is a sequence whose terms are specified by the formula $t_n = 3n - 1$. A given term can be found by subsituting the appropriate value of n into the formula. The first five terms (for $n = 1, 2, 3, 4,$ and 5) are $\{2, 5, 8, 11, 14\}$.

$t_n = \dfrac{(-1)^n}{n}$

This is another sequence whose terms are given by a formula. The $(-1)^n$ alternates the sign of successive terms because it gives -1 when n is odd and +1 when n is even. The first four terms (for $n = 1, 2, 3,$ and 4) are $\{-1, \frac{1}{2}, -\frac{1}{3}, \frac{1}{4}\}$.

Lesson Ten: Sequences and Series (cont.)

$t_1 = 3$

$t_n = 2t_{n-1} + 1 \quad (n > 1)$

This sequence is defined recursively, i.e. each term (except the first term) is defined in terms of the previous one. The first five terms of this sequence are $\{3, 7, 15, 31, 63\}$.

Some types of infinite sequences may approach a **limiting value**. For example, the sequence given by $1/n^2$ has the limit zero as n approaches infinity. The sequence given by $(1 + 1/n)^n$ is even more interesting. It gets closer and closer to the value of e (2.71828...) as n gets larger and larger.

Two special types of sequences are investigated below.

Arithmetic Sequences

An **arithmetic sequence** is a sequence in which each term differs from the previous one by a common difference. Each term in the sequence can be found from a formula like the one below.

$t_n = t_1 + (n - 1)d$

In this formula, t_1 is the first term, t_n is the nth term, and d is the difference between successive terms. To find the nth term, you simply specify a value for n and calculate.

Examples:

1) An arithmetic sequence has $t_1 = 5$ and $d = 6$. Write the first four terms.

   $t_1 = 5$

   $t_2 = t_1 + (2 - 1)d = 5 + (2 - 1)6 = 11$

   $t_3 = t_1 + (3 - 1)d = 5 + (3 - 1)6 = 17$

   $t_4 = t_1 + (4 - 1)d = 5 + (4 - 1)6 = 23$

2) An arithmetic sequence has 3 as its first term and a difference of 4 between successive terms. What is the fifth term?

   $t_n = t_1 + (n - 1)d$

   $t_5 = 3 + (5 - 1)4$

   $= 19$

Lesson Ten: Sequences and Series (cont.)

Geometric Sequences

A **geometric sequence** is a sequence that has a common ratio between successive terms. Each term is some number times the preceding term. A given term (the nth term) in the sequence can be found from a formula like the one below.

$$t_n = t_1 r^{n-1}$$

The t_n is the nth term in this formula, t_1 is the first term, and r is the ratio of a term to the preceding one.

Examples:

1) A geometric sequence has $t_1 = 2$ and $r = 3$. Write the first four terms.

$$t_1 = 2$$

$$t_2 = t_1 r^{2-1} = 2 \cdot 3^{2-1} = 6$$

$$t_3 = t_1 r^{3-1} = 2 \cdot 3^{3-1} = 18$$

$$t_4 = t_1 r^{4-1} = 2 \cdot 3^{4-1} = 54$$

2) A geometric sequence has 3 as its first term and a ratio of 2 between successive terms. What is the fifth term?

$$t_n = t_1 r^{n-1}$$

$$t_5 = 3 \cdot 2^{5-1} = 48$$

Lesson Ten: Sequences and Series (cont.)

SERIES

The sum of the terms in a sequence is called a **series**. A series may be represented as a list of terms with plus signs to indicate the addition or a formula that indicates the sum of the terms.

Sometimes a special **summation notation**, called the **sigma notation**, is introduced to indicate the sum of a set of terms. The sigma notation consists of a large Greek letter, sigma ($\sum$), followed by a formula. Immediately below the sigma, there is usually a variable, followed by an equal sign and a value. This variable is sometimes called the **summation variable**, and it is usually an integer. Another value is present above the sigma. The formula contains the summation variable, either as part of a term or as a subscript to another variable. Four examples are shown below.

$$\sum_{i=1}^{5} t_i \qquad \sum_{k=1}^{4} \frac{k}{k+1} \qquad \sum_{k=1}^{n} \frac{1}{k} \qquad \sum_{k=1}^{\infty} \frac{1}{k^2}$$

The sigma notation specifies a sum. The first term in the sum has the summation variable set to the value that is under the sigma. In each succeeding term, the summation variable is increased by 1. The last term in the sum has the summation variable equal to the value above the sigma.

In the first example above, the summation variable is i, its first (or initial) value is 1, and its last (or final) value is 5. The summation could be expanded as is shown below.

$$\sum_{i=1}^{5} t_i = t_1 + t_2 + t_3 + t_4 + t_5$$

In the second example, the summation variable, k, goes from 1 to 4, and the summation could be expanded as follows.

$$\sum_{k=1}^{4} \frac{k}{k+1} = \frac{1}{2} + \frac{2}{3} + \frac{3}{4} + \frac{4}{5}$$

The third example specifies a sum going from $k = 1$ to $k =$ **some arbitrary n value**. It can be expanded as follows.

$$\sum_{k=1}^{n} \frac{1}{k} = \frac{1}{1} + \frac{1}{2} + \frac{1}{3} + \dots + \frac{1}{n}$$

Lesson Ten: Sequences and Series (cont.)

The last example shows how an infinite series could be specified. In this case, k goes from 1 to infinity, and the expansion could be written as follows.

$$\sum_{k=1}^{\infty} \frac{1}{k^2} = \frac{1}{1} + \frac{1}{4} + \frac{1}{9} + \ldots + \frac{1}{k^2} + \ldots$$

Arithmetic Series

It is interesting to look at the sums of an arithmetic sequence and a geometric sequence. The sum of the terms in an arithmetic sequence is called an **arithmetic series**. It can be written as follows (for n terms).

$$S_n = t_1 + (k-1)d$$

$$= t_1 + (t_1 + d) + (t_1 + 2d) + (t_1 + 3d) + \ldots + (t_1 + (n-2)d) + (t_1 + (n-1)d)$$

Some simple manipulations can be used to find a formula that gives the sum of the terms. First, write the sum and then write it again with the terms in reverse order.

$$S_n = t_1 + (t_1 + d) + (t_1 + 2d) + \ldots + (t_1 + (n-3)d) + (t_1 + (n-2)d) + (t_1 + (n-1)d)$$

$$S_n = (t_1 + (n-1)d) + (t_1 + (n-2)d) + (t_1 + (n-3)d) + \ldots + (t_1 + 2d) + (t_1 + d) + t_1$$

Next, add the two equations. This will give $2S_n$ on the left.

$$2S_n = [t_1 + (t_1 + (n-1)d)] + [(t_1 + d) + (t_1 + (n-2)d)] + [(t_1 + 2d) + (t_1 + (n-3)d)]$$
$$+ \ldots + [(t_1 + (n-3)d) + (t_1 + 2d)] + [(t_1 + (n-2)d) + (t_1 + d)]$$
$$+ [(t_1 + (n-1)d) + t_1]$$

$$= [2t_1 + (n-1)d] + [2t_1 + (n-1)d] + [2t_1 + (n-1)d] + \ldots + [2t_1 + (n-1)d]$$
$$+ [2t_1 + (n-1)d] + [2t_1 + (n-1)d]$$

$$= n[2t_1 + (n-1)d]$$

Solving for S_n gives the formula for the sum of n terms of an arithmetic series.

$$S_n = \frac{n}{2}[2t_1 + (n-1)d]$$

Lesson Ten: Sequences and Series (cont.)

The following examples show some arithmetic series and their sums.

Examples:

1) Write the first five terms of an arithmetic series whose first term is $t_1 = 5$ and whose difference is $d = 3$. Also calculate the sum of the first five terms using the formula.

$$S_5 = t_1 + [t_1 + (2 - 1)d] + [t_1 + (3 - 1)d] + [t_1 + (4 - 1)d] + [t_1 + (5 - 1)d]$$

$$= 5 + [5 + 1(3)] + [5 + 2(3)] + [5 + 3(3)] + [5 + 4(3)]$$

$$= 5 + 8 + 11 + 14 + 17$$

$$= \tfrac{5}{2}[2t_1 + (5 - 1)d]$$

$$= \tfrac{5}{2}[2(5) + 4(3)]$$

$$= 55$$

2) Write the first six terms and find the sum of the first six terms of an arithmetic series whose first term is $t_1 = 1$ and whose difference is $d = \tfrac{1}{2}$.

$$S_6 = t_1 + [t_1 + (2 - 1)\tfrac{1}{2}] + [t_1 + (3 - 1)\tfrac{1}{2}] + [t_1 + (4 - 1)\tfrac{1}{2}] + [t_1 + (5 - 1)\tfrac{1}{2}]$$
$$+ [t_1 + (6 - 1)\tfrac{1}{2}]$$

$$= 1 + [1 + \tfrac{1}{2}] + [1 + 1] + [1 + \tfrac{3}{2}] + [1 + 2] + [1 + \tfrac{5}{2}]$$

$$= 1 + 1.5 + 2 + 2.5 + 3 + 3.5$$

$$= \tfrac{6}{2}[2t_1 + (6 - 1)d]$$

$$= 3[2(1) + 5(\tfrac{1}{2})]$$

$$= 3 \cdot 4.5$$

$$= 13.5$$

Lesson Ten: Sequences and Series (cont.)

Geometric Series

The sum of the terms in a geometric sequence is called a **geometric series** and can be written (for n terms) as shown below.

$$S_n = t_1 r^{k-1}$$

$$= t_1 + t_1 r^1 + t_1 r^2 + t_1 r^3 + \dots + t_1 r^{n-2} + t_1 r^{n-1}$$

You will recall that t_1 is the first term in the sequence and that r is the ratio between adjacent terms.

A formula for the sum of series can be found writing the first n terms of the series and then writing them again multiplied by r.

$$S_n = t_1 + t_1 r^1 + t_1 r^2 + t_1 r^3 + \dots + t_1 r^{n-2} + t_1 r^{n-1}$$

$$rS_n = rt_1 + t_1 r^2 + t_1 r^3 + t_1 r^4 + \dots + t_1 r^{n-2} + t_1 r^{n-1} + t_1 r^n$$

Subtracting the second equation from the first one gives the following expression.

$$S_n - rS_n = t_1 - t_1 r^n$$

Factoring both sides and then solving the resulting equation for S_n gives a formula for the first n terms of a geometric series.

$$S_n(1 - r) = t_1(1 - r^n)$$

$$S_n = \frac{t_1(1 - r^n)}{1 - r}$$

The following examples show some geometric series and their sums.

Examples:

1) Write the first four terms of a geometric series whose first term is $t_1 = 2$ and whose ratio is $r = 3$. Also calculate the sum of the first four terms using the formula.

$$S_n = t_1 + t_1 r^{2-1} + t_1 r^{3-1} + t_1 r^{4-1}$$

$$= 2 + 2(3) + 2(3)^2 + 2(3)^3$$

$$= 2 + 6 + 18 + 54$$

$$= \frac{t_1(1 - r^4)}{1 - r} = \frac{2(1 - 3^4)}{1 - 3} = 80$$

Lesson Ten: Sequences and Series (cont.)

2) Write the first six terms of a geometric series whose first term is $t_1 = 16$ and whose ratio is $r = \frac{1}{2}$. Also calculate the sum of the first six terms using the formula.

$$S_6 = t_1 + t_1 r^{2-1} + t_1 r^{3-1} + t_1 r^{4-1} + t_1 r^{5-1} + t_1 r^{6-1}$$

$$= 16 + 16\left(\tfrac{1}{2}\right) + 16\left(\tfrac{1}{2}\right)^2 + 16\left(\tfrac{1}{2}\right)^3 + 16\left(\tfrac{1}{2}\right)^4 + 16\left(\tfrac{1}{2}\right)^5$$

$$= 16 + 8 + 4 + 2 + 1 + \tfrac{1}{2}$$

$$= \frac{t_1(1 - r^6)}{1 - r} \qquad = \qquad \frac{16(1 - \frac{1}{64})}{1 - \frac{1}{2}} \qquad = \tfrac{63}{2}$$

THE BINOMIAL THEOREM

There are many occasions in mathematics when you need to take a sum of two terms to a non-negative integer power, $(a + b)^n$. You can do this, of course, by repeatedly multiplying by the sum of the terms, but this process can quickly become tedious and error-prone. A better method is to use the **binomial theorem**.

The binomial theorem can be written as follows.

$$(a + b)^n = a^n + \frac{n!}{1!(n-1)!}\, a^{n-1}b + \frac{n!}{2!(n-2)!}\, a^{n-2}b^2$$

$$+ \frac{n!}{3!(n-3)!}\, a^{n-3}b^3 + \ldots + \frac{n!}{r!(n-r)!}\, a^{n-r}b^r + \ldots$$

$$+ \frac{n!}{(n-2)2!}\, a^2 b^{n-2} + \frac{n!}{(n-1)!\, 1!}\, ab^{n-1} + b^n$$

The quantities that are followed by exclamation marks are integer quantities that are called factorials. A **factorial** is the product of all the positive integers from the one preceding the exclamation mark down to 1. It is usually identified as the quantity followed by the word *factorial*. For example, **5!** is called "five factorial," and $n!$ is called "n factorial." Zero factorial (0!) and one factorial (1!) are both defined to be 1. Some factorials, along with the way that they are computed, are shown below.

$$0! = 1 \qquad\qquad\qquad\qquad 1! = 1$$

$$3! = 3 \cdot 2 \cdot 1 = 6 \qquad\qquad 5! = 5 \cdot 4 \cdot 3 \cdot 2 \cdot 1 = 120$$

$$n! = n \cdot (n-1) \cdot (n-2) \cdot \ldots \cdot 1$$

$$(n-3)! = (n-3) \cdot (n-4) \cdot (n-5) \cdot \ldots \cdot 1$$

Lesson Ten: Sequences and Series (cont.)

In the binomial formula, each term except the first one and the last one is preceded by a coefficient that is found by dividing a factorial by two other factorials. The n value in the upper factorial is the power to which $(a + b)$ is taken, and the r value that appears in the lower ones is the number of the term. The leftmost term has $r = 0$, the next one to the right has $r = 1$, the next one to the right has $r = 2$, and so on. The rightmost term has $r = n$. Two other things should be noted: (1) $(a + b)^n$ always produces n terms, and (2) in each term, the powers of a and b add up to n.

The examples below show how the binomial theorem can be used to find the sum of two terms to a non-negative power. It can also be used to find the <u>difference</u> of two terms to a non-negative power, if the difference is expressed as follows: $(a - b)^n = (a + -b)^n$.

1. $(x + 2)^0 = 1$

$$(x + 3)^3 = x^3 + \frac{3!}{1!(3 - 1)!} \, x^2 \cdot 3 + \frac{3!}{2!(3 - 2)!} \, x \cdot 3^2 + 3^3$$

$$= x^3 + \frac{3 \cdot 2 \cdot 1}{1(2 \cdot 1)} \, x^2 \cdot 3 + \frac{3 \cdot 2 \cdot 1}{2 \cdot 1(1)} \, x \cdot 9 + 27$$

$$= x^3 + 3 \cdot x^2 \cdot 3 + 3 \cdot x \cdot 9 + 27$$

$$= x^3 + 9x^2 + 27x + 27$$

2. $(x + b)^4 = x^4 + \dfrac{4!}{1!(4 - 1)!} \, x^3 b + \dfrac{4!}{2!(4 - 2)!} \, x^2 b^2 + \dfrac{4!}{3!(4 - 3)!} \, x b^3 + b^4$

$$= x^4 + \frac{4 \cdot 3 \cdot 2 \cdot 1}{1(3 \cdot 2 \cdot 1)} \, x^3 b + \frac{4 \cdot 3 \cdot 2 \cdot 1}{(2 \cdot 1)(2 \cdot 1)} \, x^2 b^2 + \frac{4 \cdot 3 \cdot 2 \cdot 1}{(3 \cdot 2 \cdot 1)(1)} \, x b^3 + b^4$$

$$= x^4 + 4x^3 b + 6x^2 b^2 + 4x b^3 + b^4$$

3. $(x - 2)^4 = x^4 + \dfrac{4!}{1!\,(4 - 1)!} \, x^3 (-2) + \dfrac{4!}{2!\,(4 - 2)!} \, x^2 (-2)^2 + \dfrac{4!}{3!\,(4 - 3)!} \, x (-2)^3 + (-2)^4$

$$= x^4 + \frac{4 \cdot 3 \cdot 2 \cdot 1}{1(3 \cdot 2 \cdot 1)} \, x^3 (-2) + \frac{4 \cdot 3 \cdot 2 \cdot 1}{(2 \cdot 1)(2 \cdot 1)} \, x^2 (-2)^2 + \frac{4 \cdot 3 \cdot 2 \cdot 1}{(3 \cdot 2 \cdot 1)(1)} \, x (-2)^3 + (-2)^4$$

$$= x^4 + 4x^3 (-2) + 6x^2 (4) + 4x (-8) + 16$$

$$= x^4 - 8x^3 + 24x^2 - 32x + 16$$

Name: _____ Date: _____

Lesson Ten: Exercises

Complete the following exercises on your own paper.

1. Find the next three terms in the following sequences.

a) 1, 3, 5, 7

b) 2, 4, 6, 8

c) 2, 4, 8, 16, 32

d) $\frac{1}{2}, \frac{1}{4}, \frac{1}{6}, \frac{1}{8}$

e) $\frac{1}{2}, \frac{1}{5}, \frac{1}{10}, \frac{1}{17}$

f) 1, -3, 5, -7, 9, -11

2. Identify the following sequences as finite or infinite.

a) {1, 4, 9, 16, 25}

b) {1, 4, 7, 10, ...}

c) $\{t_n = 5n + 2 \mid n = 1, 2, 3\}$

d) The odd positive integers less than 10

e) The squares of all of the positive integers

f) The positive integers that are evenly divisible by 4

3. The domains of the following finite sequences consist of the integers $n = 1, 2, 3, 4$. Write the four terms of each of the sequences.

a) $t_n = 3n + 1$

b) $t_n = 16 - n^2$

c) $t_n = \frac{1}{n^3}$

d) $t_n = (-1)^n$

e) $t_n = \frac{1}{(-3)^n}$

f) $t_n = n^2 - n$

4. The following infinite sequences are defined by their first two terms and a formula for their general term. Write the third, fourth, and fifth terms.

a) 0, 2, ..., $2n - 2$, ...

b) 3, 12, ..., $3n^2$, ...

c) 0, $\frac{1}{3}$, ..., $\frac{n-1}{n+1}$, ...

d) $\frac{1}{2}, \frac{4}{3}, ..., \frac{n^2}{(n+1)}$, ...

e) $\frac{1}{2}, \frac{1}{4}, ..., \frac{1}{2^n}$, ...

f) $\frac{1}{2}, \frac{1}{2}, ..., \frac{n}{2^n}$, ...

g) -1, $\frac{1}{2}$, ..., $\frac{(-1)^n}{n}$, ...

h) 0, 3, ..., $n + (-1)^n$, ...

i) 0, $\frac{9}{16}$, ..., $(1 - \frac{1}{n^n})^n$, ...

Name: _____ Date: _____

Lesson Ten: Exercises (cont.)

5. The following formulas define infinite sequences for $n = 1, 2, 3, \ldots$. Find the first four terms of each sequence.

a) $t_n = 3n - 5$ **b)** $t_n = n^n$ **c)** $t_n = n - \dfrac{1}{n}$

d) $t_n = \dfrac{n-1}{(-2)^{n-1}}$ **e)** $t_n = \dfrac{n+1}{2n-1}$ **f)** $t_n = \dfrac{n}{n+1} + \dfrac{n+1}{n}$

6. The following infinite sequences are defined recursively. Find the second, third, fourth, and fifth term of each sequence.

a) $t_1 = 0$, $t_n = 3 + t_{n-1}$ **b)** $t_1 = 1$, $t_n = 2t_{n-1}$

c) $t_1 = 2$, $t_n = nt_{n-1}$ **d)** $t_1 = 1$, $t_n = (-1)^n t_{n-1}$

e) $t_1 = 2$, $t_n = \dfrac{t_{n-1}}{n}$ **f)** $t_1 = 2$, $t_n = \dfrac{t_{n-1}^2}{2}$

7. Find the limit of the following sequences as n becomes larger and larger.

a) $t_n = \dfrac{1}{n}$ **b)** $t_n = \dfrac{6}{(n-1)}$

c) $t_n = \dfrac{1-n}{(n+1)}$ **d)** $t_n = 2 + \dfrac{1}{n}$

e) $t_n = (1 + \dfrac{1}{n})^n$ **f)** $t_n = \dfrac{n-1}{n(n+1)}$

8. Find the second, third, fourth, and fifth terms of the following arithmetic sequences.

a) $t_1 = 0$, $d = 1$ **b)** $t_1 = 1$, $d = 4$ **c)** $t_1 = 3$, $d = 2$

d) $t_1 = 0$, $d = 10$ **e)** $t_1 = 5$, $d = 5$ **f)** $t_1 = -2$, $d = 4$

Name: _____ Date: _____

Lesson Ten: Exercises (cont.)

9. Find the second, third, fourth, and fifth terms of the following geometric sequences.

a) $t_1 = 1, r = 1$

b) $t_1 = 1, r = 2$

c) $t_1 = 2, r = 2$

d) $t_1 = 1, r = 10$

e) $t_1 = 5, r = 5$

f) $t_1 = 2, r = 4$

10. Find the sum of the terms in the following series.

a) $\displaystyle\sum_{k=1}^{4} \frac{1}{k}$

b) $\displaystyle\sum_{k=1}^{3} \frac{1}{k^2}$

c) $\displaystyle\sum_{k=0}^{5} k^2$

d) $\displaystyle\sum_{k=1}^{6} 2(k-1)$

e) $\displaystyle\sum_{k=0}^{6} k(k-1)$

f) $\displaystyle\sum_{k=2}^{5} \frac{k}{k+1}$

11. Find the sums of the terms in the following arithmetic series.

a) $S_n = 1 + (k-1)2, n = 5$

b) $\displaystyle\sum_{k=1}^{6} 1 + (k-1)2$

c) $S_n = 2 + 3(k-1), n = 8$

d) $\displaystyle\sum_{k=1}^{8} 3 + (k-1)5$

e) $t_1 = 4, d = 3, n = 10$

f) $t_1 = 2, d = 6, n = 15$

g) $t_1 = 5, d = 5, n = 20$

h) $t_1 = 5, d = 10, n = 50$

Name: _____ Date: _____

Lesson Ten: Exercises (cont.)

12. Find the sums of the terms in the following geometric series.

a) $S_n = 1 \cdot 2^{n-1}$ $\quad n = 4$

b) $\displaystyle\sum_{k=1}^{4} 1 \cdot 2^{k-1}$

c) $S_n = 3 \cdot 2^{n-1}$ $\quad n = 5$

d) $\displaystyle\sum_{k=1}^{8} 2 \cdot 3^{k-1}$

e) $t_1 = 1$, $r = 5$, $n = 6$

f) $t_1 = 2$, $r = \frac{1}{2}$, $n = 10$

g) $t_1 = 4$, $r = \frac{1}{3}$, $n = 5$

h) $t_1 = 2$, $r = \frac{1}{4}$, $n = 20$

13. Find the following binomial expansions.

a) $(x + y)^0$

b) $(a + b)^1$

c) $(x + y)^2$

d) $(a + b)^3$

e) $(x + y)^5$

f) $(x + y)^6$

g) $(x + 2)^6$

h) $(x - 2)^6$

Pre-Calculus Vocabulary

Students can use the following list as a review and study tool. They can look up each term as that lesson is completed and study the vocabulary before a test is given.

Lesson One:
Cardinal Numbers
Ordinal Numbers
Nominal Numbers
Counting Numbers
Natural Numbers
Set
Element or Member
Whole Numbers
Subset
Integers
Positive Integers
Negative Integers
Absolute Value
Rational Number
Terminate
Repeating Decimal
Irrational Numbers
Real Numbers
Complex Numbers
Real Part
Imaginary Part
Complex Conjugate
Modulus

Lesson Two:
Linear Equation
First-degree Equation
Slope
Vertical Intercept
y-intercept
Horizontal Intercept
x-intercept
Rise
Run
Slope-Intercept Form
Point-Slope Form
General Linear Equation Form
Intercept Form
Parallel

Perpendicular
Function
Domain
Range
Evaluating the Function

Lesson Three:
Greater Than
Less Than
Greater Than or Equal To
Less Than or Equal To
Inequalities
Intervals
Open Interval
Closed Interval
Unbounded
Bounded
Definition of $a < b$
Trichotomy Property
Addition Order Property
Multiplication Order Property
Transitive Order Property
Addition Property
Multiplication Property
Reciprocal Property
Half-Planes
Absolute Value Function
Step Function

Lesson Four:
Non-linear
Quadratics
Quadratic Function
Quadratic Equation
Parabola
Symmetric
Vertex
Roots
Factoring
Completing the Square

Quadratic Formula
Discriminant

Lesson Five:
Polynomial
Term
Degree
Coefficients
Monomial
Binomial
Trinomial
Standard Form
Constant Term
Factoring
Inspection
Difference of Two Squares
Difference of Two Cubes
Sum of Two Cubes
Difference of Two nth Powers
Grouping
Factor Theorem
Partial Fractions
Partial Fraction Decomposition
Rational Expressions

Lesson Six:
Exponential Function
Exponent
Base
e
Logarithm
Antilogarithm
Common Logarithms
Natural Logarithms

Pre-Calculus Vocabulary (cont.)

Lesson Seven:
Angle
Vertex
Degree
Relatively
Absolutely
Right Angle
Perpendicular
Straight Angle
Acute Angle
Obtuse Angle
Reflex Angle
Radian
Subtends
Trigonometric Functions
Quadrants
Sine
Amplitude
Period
Phase
Cosine
Tangent
Cosecant
Secant
Cotangent
Trigonometric Identity
Inverse Trigonometric Functions
Arcsin (Inverse Sine)
Arccos (Inverse Cosine)
Arctan (Inverse Tangent)

Lesson Eight:
Right Triangle
Hypotenuse
The Pythagorean Theorem
The Sum of the Angles in a Triangle
The Sine, Cosine, and Tangent Functions
Sum and Difference of Angles Formulas
Double Angle Formulas
Half Angle Formulas

Lesson Nine:
Real Roots
Fundamental Theorem of Algebra
N-Roots Theorem
Symmetry
Scaling
Translating
Absolute Value Functions
Slope
Concavity
Concave Upward
Concave Downward
Inflection Points
Relative Maximum (Local Maximum)
Relative Minimum (Local Minimum)
Absolute Maximum
Absolute Minimum
Asymptote
Rational Function
Linear Axis
Log Axis
Log-Linear Graph
Log-Log Graph
Polar Coordinates
Positive Polar Axis

Lesson Ten:
Sequence
Terms
Limiting Value
Arithmetic Sequence
Geometric Sequence
Series
Summation Notation
Sigma Notation
Summation Variable
Arithmetic Series
Geometric Series
Binomial Theorem
Factorial

Answer Keys

*Teachers should check all graphs. Space limitations do not allow for the inclusion of answer keys for graphs.

Lesson One (pages 8–12)

1.
- **a)** cardinal **b)** ordinal **c)** nominal
- **d)** nominal **e)** ordinal **f)** cardinal

2.
- **a)** whole numbers **b)** natural numbers
- **c)** integers

3.
- **a)** $\{1, 2, 3\}$ **b)** $\{4, 5, 6, 7, 8\}$
- **c)** $\{0, 1, 2, 3, 4\}$ **d)** $\{5, 6, 7, 8, 9\}$
- **e)** $\{1, 2, 3\}$ **f)** $\{-3, -2, -1\}$

4.
- **a)** F **b)** T **c)** F **d)** F **e)** T

5.
- **a)** $\frac{1}{2}$ **b)** $\frac{1}{8}$ **c)** $\frac{9}{4}$ **d)** $\frac{5}{3}$
- **e)** $\frac{9}{5}$ **f)** $\frac{12}{5}$ **g)** $\frac{7}{6}$ **h)** $\frac{7}{3}$

6.

$\frac{1}{9} = 0.111111111$ $\frac{2}{9} = 0.222222222$

$\frac{3}{9} = 0.333333333$ $\frac{4}{9} = 0.444444444$

$\frac{5}{9} = 0.555555555$ $\frac{6}{9} = 0.666666666$

$\frac{7}{9} = 0.777777777$ $\frac{8}{9} = 0.888888888$

7.

all irrational
- **a)** 2.645751311 **b)** 3.316624790
- **c)** 2.236067977 **d)** 4.123105626
- **e)** 4.358898944

8.
- **a)** associative addition
- **b)** associative multiplication
- **c)** multiplication property
- **d)** distributive property
- **e)** multiplicative inverse
- **f)** commutative addition

9.
- **a)** $16.0/(4.0/2.0) = 8.0$ $(16.0/4.0)/2.0 = 2.0$
- **b)** $6.6/3.3 = 2.0$ $3.3/6.6 = 0.5$
- **c)** $2.5 - 1.3 = 1.2$ $1.3 - 2.5 = -1.2$

10.
- **a)** 12 **b)** 167 **c)** 125.25
- **d)** 15.67 **e)** 0.125

11.
- **a)** 5 **b)** 13 **c)** 3.61 **d)** 6.77

12.
- **a)** $4 + 3i$ **b)** $-12 - 5i$
- **c)** $2 - 3i$ **d)** $2.2 - 6.4i$

13.
- **a)** $3 + 5i$ **b)** $10 - 8i$
- **c)** $12 - 5i$ **d)** $6 + 8i$
- **e)** $2 - 2i$ **f)** $-2 - 7i$
- **g)** $-2 + 7i$ **h)** $4 - 8i$
- **i)** $13.6 - 4.4i$

14.
- **a)** $1 + i$ **b)** $2 - 2i$
- **c)** $4 + i$ **d)** $-2 - 2i$
- **e)** $10 - 8i$ **f)** $16 + 7i$
- **g)** $-4 - 3i$ **h)** $-4 - 2i$
- **i)** $4.8 + 1.6i$

15.
- **a)** $7 + 4i$ **b)** $39 - 2i$
- **c)** $26 - 32i$ **d)** $1 + 8i$
- **e)** $-9 + 38i$ **f)** $-38 + 16i$
- **g)** $10 - 5i$ **h)** $35 + 42i$
- **i)** $6.82 - 23.33i$

16.
- **a)** $-0.5 - 2.5i$ **b)** $2.25 + 0.25i$
- **c)** $1.52 + 0.64i$ **d)** $1.8 - 3.4i$
- **e)** $0.5 + 2i$ **f)** $1.69 + 0.46i$
- **g)** $4 - 2i$ **h)** $5.54 - 3.69i$
- **i)** $1 + 0.722i$

Lesson Two (pages 19–20)

4.
- **a)** $y = 3x + 4$ **b)** $y = -\frac{1}{4}x + \frac{1}{2}$
- **c)** $y = -4x - 6$ **d)** $y = \frac{1}{2}x - 2$
- **e)** $y = 1.25x - 5.5$ **f)** $y = 3$

5.
- **a)** $y - 1 = 2(x - 1)$ **b)** $y - 2 = -3(x + 3)$
  $y = 2x - 1$ $y = -3x - 7$

- **c)** $y - 0.5 = -0.5(x - 2)$ **d)** $y - 3 = \frac{4}{3}(x + 6)$
  $y = -0.5x + 1.5$ $y = \frac{4}{3}x + 11$

- **e)** $y - 0 = 8(x - 0)$ **f)** $y - \frac{3}{5} = 1(x + \frac{3}{4})$
  $y = 8x$ $y = x + \frac{27}{20}$

6.

a) $\dfrac{y-1}{-1-1} = \dfrac{x-1}{-1-1}$
$y = x$

b) $\dfrac{y-0}{-2-0} = \dfrac{x-2}{0-2}$
$y = x - 2$

c) $\dfrac{y-2}{4-2} = \dfrac{x-4}{2-4}$
$y = -x + 6$

d) $\dfrac{y-2}{-\frac{3}{2}-2} = \dfrac{x-\frac{1}{2}}{-4-\frac{1}{2}}$
$y = \frac{7}{9}x + \frac{29}{18}$

e) $\dfrac{y-13}{-1-13} = \dfrac{x-1}{8-1}$
$y = -2x + 15$

f) $\dfrac{y-2}{0-2} = \dfrac{x-5}{0-5}$
$y = \frac{2}{5}x$

7.

a) $m = -2$ b) $m = -\frac{4}{5}$
c) $m = 9$ d) $m = \frac{1}{2}$
e) $m = 2$ f) $m = -1$

8.

a) $b = 2$ b) $b = \frac{11}{5}$
c) $b = -6$ d) $b = 19$
e) $b = -\frac{13}{3}$ f) $b = 18$

9.

a) $a = 2$ b) $a = -\frac{8}{3}$
c) $a = \frac{5}{2}$ d) $a = -3$
e) $a = \frac{13}{6}$ f) $a = 18$

10.

a) $y = -2x + 4$ b) $y = 3x + 5$
c) $y = -\frac{5}{4}x + \frac{1}{2}$

11.

a) $\frac{y}{1} + \frac{x}{2} = 1$ b) $\frac{y}{6} + -\frac{x}{9} = 1$
c) $\frac{y}{2} + \frac{x}{4} = 1$

12.

a) $m = -2$ b) $m = 5$
c) $m = 0.5$

13.

a) not parallel   b) parallel
c) parallel

14.

a) $f(2) = -9, f(5) = -27, f(-3) = 21$
b) $f(1) = 2, f(-5) = -40, f(6) = 37$
c) $f(2) = 2.5, f(-3) = 0, f(0.5) = 1.75$
d) $f(-4) = -6, f(0) = 6, f(3) = 15$
e) $f(-1.5) = -0.5, f(2.5) = 3.5, f(10) = 11$
f) $f(2) = 1.75, f(2.5) = 3.5, f(-1.5) = -10.5$

Lesson Three (pages 28–29)

1.

2.

a) $x \le -2$ b) $x > -1$
c) $-2 < x \le 5$ d) $4 \le x \le 8$
e) $-1 < x < 1$ f) $6 \le x < 9$

3.

a) y   b) z   c) x   d) x
e) y   f) z   g) x

5.

a) $x \ge 5$ b) $x \le 4$
c) $x < -2$ d) $x \ge \frac{5}{2}$
e) $x \ge -\frac{5}{3}$ f) $x > \frac{12}{5}$
g) $x \le -4$ h) $x \le 3$
i) $x > -10$

Lesson Four (page 37)

2.

  a) $x = -1$, $x = -1$ (double root)
  b) $x = 2$, $x = 4$
  c) $x = \frac{1}{2}$, $x = -\frac{1}{2}$
  d) $x = \frac{1}{2}$, $x = -\frac{3}{2}$
  e) $x = -3$, $x = -1$
  f) $x = 5$, $x = 5$ (double root)
  g) $x = 0$, $x = 6$
  h) $x = 0$, $x = -\frac{4}{5}$
  i) $x = 0$, $x = 0$ (double root)

3.

  a) $x = -7$, $x = 1$
  b) $x = -3$, $x = -1$
  c) $x = \frac{1}{3}$, $x = \frac{1}{2}$
  d) $x = \frac{1}{2}$, $x = -1$
  e) $x = -1$, $x = 6$
  f) $x = 2 + \sqrt{3}$, $x = 2 - \sqrt{3}$

4.

  a) $x = -3$, $x = -4$
  b) $x = \frac{1}{3}$, $x = -\frac{1}{2}$
  c) $x = 5$, $x = 5$ (double root)
  d) $x = -\frac{1}{2} + \sqrt{\frac{13}{4}}$, $x = -\frac{1}{2} - \sqrt{\frac{13}{4}}$ or
      $x = -\frac{1}{2} + \frac{\sqrt{13}}{2}$, $x = -\frac{1}{2} - \frac{\sqrt{13}}{2}$
  e) $x = 1 + 2i$, $x = 1 - 2i$
  f) $x = -\frac{1}{2} + \frac{1}{2}i$, $x = -\frac{1}{2} - \frac{1}{2}i$

Lesson Five (pages 51–54)

1.

  a) trinomial   **b)** binomial
  c) monomial   **d)** trinomial
  e) monomial   **f)** binomial

2.

  a) $-4x^4 + 7x^3 + x^2 + 6x - 2$
  b) $6x^3 - 11x^2 - x + 5$
  c) $4x^5 - 3x^3 + 3x^2 - 11$
  d) $2x^3 - 6x + 14$

3.

  a) 1   **b)** 1   **c)** 1   **d)** 1

4.

  a) $3x^2 + x + 9$
  b) $2x^2 + 5x + 2$
  c) $5x^3 + x^2 - x + 4$
  d) $x^3 - 8x^2 + 2x - 4$
  e) $3x^4 - 2x^3 + 3x^2 + x - 14$
  f) $3x^4 - 2x^3 - 3x^2 - 6x + 11$

  g) $3x^4 + 3x^3 + 3x^2 + 2x + 5$
  h) $3x^5 + 4x^3 + 2x^2 + 4x + 5$

5.

  a) $6x^2 - 13x - 5$
  b) $x^2 + 5x - 14$
  c) $6x^3 - x^2 - 9x + 4$
  d) $x^3 + 4x^2 + 5x + 6$
  e) $2x^4 - x^3 - 10x^2 + x + 2$
  f) $12x^4 + 10x^3 + 33x^2 - 4x + 24$
  g) $2x^6 + x^5 - 4x^4 + 3x^2 + 8x - 12$
  h) $2x^7 + 10x^6 + 2x^5 - 15x^4 + 39x^3 - 26x^2 + 6x + 3$

6.

  a) $x + 3$ **b)** $x - 4$
  c) $2x^3 + 3x^2 - x + 1$ **d)** $x^3 - 2x^2 + 3x + 1$
  e) $x - 3$ **f)** $x^3 + x^2 - x + 1$
  g) $x^4 - 3x^3 + 4x^2 - 7x + 2$
  h) $9x^2 + 12x - 6$

7.

  a) quotient = $3x - 6$; remainder = 8
  b) quotient = $x^2 + 6x + 9$; remainder = 25
  c) quotient = $x + 2$; remainder = 2
  d) quotient = $x^2 + 2x - 1$;
       remainder = $7x + 4$

8.

  a) $(x + 2)(x - 2)$
  b) $(2x + 3)(2x - 3)$
  c) $(2x - 5)(4x^2 + 10x + 25)$
  d) $(3x + 4)(9x^2 - 12x + 16)$
  e) $(x - 6)(x^2 + 6x + 36)$
  f) $(x - 2)(x + 2)((x^2 + 2x + 4)(x^2 - 2x + 4))$
  g) $(2x - 3)(16x^4 + 24x^3 + 36x^2 + 54x + 81)$
  h) $(x + 3)(x + 3)$
  i) $(x - 5)(x - 5)$
  j) $(x - 5)(x + 4)$
  k) $(x + 7)(x + 5)$
  l) $(x + 3)(x^2 + 9)$
  m) $x(x + 4)(x + 2)(x - 2)$
  n) $(x + 1)(x + 2)(x + 3)$
  o) $x(3x - 7)(3x - 7)$
  p) $(x + 2)(3x + 1)(2x + 1)$
  q) $x(x)(x - 3)(x - 3)$
  r) $(x - 1)(x + 1)(x + 2)$
  s) $(x + 1)(x - 1)(x^2 + 1)$

9.

a) $\dfrac{3}{x+2} + \dfrac{5}{x+5}$

b) $\dfrac{1}{x-3} + \dfrac{1}{x-7}$

c) $\dfrac{3}{3x-2} + \dfrac{2}{2x-1}$

d) $\dfrac{2}{x-1} + \dfrac{1}{x+1} + \dfrac{-1}{x+2}$

e) $\dfrac{-4}{x+1} + \dfrac{3}{x-2} + \dfrac{6}{x-4}$

f) $\dfrac{1}{x} + \dfrac{2}{x-1} - \dfrac{3}{x+2}$

10.

a) $2x + \dfrac{2}{x-1} - \dfrac{1}{x-2}$

b) $2 - \dfrac{1}{x-2} + \dfrac{1}{x+2}$

c) $2x - 1 + \dfrac{5}{x-1} + \dfrac{2}{x+3}$

11.

a) $\dfrac{x-2}{x+1}$ b) $\dfrac{1}{x+1}$

c) $\dfrac{1}{(x-1)(x-5)} = \dfrac{1}{x^2 - 6x + 5}$

d) $x - 6$

e) $\dfrac{1}{(x+3)(x+5)} = \dfrac{1}{x^2 + 8x + 15}$

f) $\dfrac{x-2}{3x(x+1)} = \dfrac{x-2}{3x^2 + 3x}$

g) $\dfrac{1}{x+1}$ h) $\dfrac{2}{x-4}$

i) $\dfrac{4}{2x+1}$ j) $\dfrac{2x^2}{x^2 - 1}$

Lesson Six (pages 64–67)

6.

$f(-1) = 0.333$
$f(-\tfrac{1}{2}) = 1$
$f(0) = 3$
$f(1) = 27$
$f(2) = 243$

7.

a) $y = 3^{5x}$ b) $y = 3^{3x}$
c) $y = 2^{3x+3}$ d) $y = 2^{-4x}$
e) $y = 5^{2x}$ f) $y = 3^{2x+1}$
g) $y = 2^{2x}$ h) $y = 2^{-x+4}$
i) $y = 4^{3x}$ j) $y = 2^{8x}$
k) $y = 3^{8x+2}$ l) $y = 5^{9x+4}$
m) $y = a^{9x}$ n) $y = b^{3x}$
o) $y = a^{-2x}$ p) $y = b^{6x}$

8.

a) $y = 3^{x}$ b) $y = 5^{-x}$
c) $y = a^{\frac{x}{2}}$ d) $y = 7^{2x}$
e) $y = 2^{\frac{x}{5}}$ f) $y = 3^{x}$
g) $y = 5^{\frac{-5x}{3}}$ h) $y = a^{\frac{-x}{2}}$
i) $y = 3^{\frac{3x}{2}}$ j) $y = 2^{\frac{-5x}{3}}$
k) $y = b^{\frac{8x}{5}}$ l) $y = b^{-x}$

9.

a) $y = \dfrac{1 - 2^{\frac{x}{2}+1} + 2^{x}}{1 - 2^{x}}$

b) $y = \dfrac{2 + 3 \cdot 2^{\frac{x}{2}} + 2^{x}}{1 - 2^{x}}$

c) $y = a^{\frac{x}{2}}$

d) $y = \dfrac{2^{3x} + 2^{2x} + 2^{\frac{3x}{2}} + 2^{\frac{x}{2}}}{1 - 2^{3x}}$

e) $y = \dfrac{1 + a^{\frac{5x}{2}}}{1 - a^{5x}}$

f) $y = \dfrac{b^2 + b^{\frac{x}{2}+1}}{b^2 - b^x}$

g) $y = \dfrac{3^{\frac{3x}{2}+1} - 3^{\frac{x}{2}+1}}{3^{3x} - 3^x}$

h) $y = \dfrac{a^{\frac{x}{2}} + b^{\frac{3x}{2}}}{a^x - b^{3x}}$

10.

$e^2 = 7.389$ $e^{1.5} = 4.482$

$e^{-2} = 0.135$ $e^0 = 1.000$

$e^{5.5} = 244.7$

11.

a) $y = e^{4x}$ **b)** $y = e^{5x+4}$

c) $y = e^{2x}$ **d)** $y = e^{3x+2}$

e) $y = e^{6x}$ **f)** $y = e^{11x+1}$

12.

a) 3   **b)** 5   **c)** 5   **d)** 3

e) -2   **f)** -4   **g)** 1   **h)** 2

i) 3   **j)** -2   **k)** 9   **l)** 7

14.

a) 8   **b)** $\frac{1}{4}$ **c)** 81   **d)** $\frac{1}{3}$

e) 1   **f)** 16   **g)** 10,000

h) $\frac{1}{10}$

15.

a) $y = \log_2 4 + \log_2 x$

b) $y = \log_4(x - 1) + \log_4(x + 10)$

c) $y = \log_{10}(x + 5) - \log_{10} x$

d) $y = \log_e x - \log_e 10$

e) $y = \log_3 5 + \log_3 x - \log_3 2$

f) $y = \log_5 x + \log_5(x + 1) - \log_5 2$

16.

a) $y = \log_5 x(x + 5)$

b) $y = \log_e 12x$

c) $y = \log_3 \frac{x}{4}$

d) $y = \log_{10}\left(\dfrac{x}{x - 1}\right)$

e) $y = \log_2 12x$

f) $y = \log_2 \left(\dfrac{5x}{3}\right)$

17.

a) $y = 4\log_{10} x$

b) $y = 7\log_2 x$

c) $y = -5\log_3 x$

d) $y = 3\log_e 2x$

e) $y = 3\log_4 x - 3\log_4 5$

f) $y = 3\log_2 x - 2\log_2 5$

18.

a) 0.898   **b)** 1.398   **c)** -0.602

d) 3.113   **e)** 0.000

19.

a) 6,025.6

b) 1,000,000,000,000

c) 0.000000001

d) 0.316

e) 1

20.

a) 2.067   **b)** 3.219   **c)** -1.386

d) 7.169   **e)** 0.000

21.

a) 43.816   **b)** 162,754.8

c) 0.000123   **d)** 0.606

e) 1.000

Lesson Seven (pages 76–77)

2.

a) acute   **b)** obtuse

c) obtuse   **d)** reflex

e) acute   **f)** acute

3.

a) 14.3°   **b)** 45°   **c)** 120°

d) 28.7°   **e)** 270°   **f)** 114.6°

4.

a) 0.524   **b)** 1.05   **c)** 0.785

d) 5.50   **e)** 6.02   **f)** 3.32

5.

0.5 radians = 28.65°

6.

0.75 radians = 43°

7.

9 inches

8.

6.25 cm

14.
  a) neg. III, IV **b)** neg. II, III
      pos. I, II   pos. I, IV
  c) neg. II, IV
      pos. I, III

16.
  a) 1.414   **b)** 1.000
  c) 1.155   **d)** 2.000
  e) 2.145   **f)** 0.176

18.
  a) -90° or 270°
  b) 0°
  c) 90
  d) -35.3° or 324.7° or 215.3°
  e) 315° or 225° or -45°
  f) 30° or 150°
  g) 5.02° or 174.98°
  h) 60° or 120°

19.
  a) 60° or 300°
  b) 90° or 270°
  c) 0°
  d) 120° or 240°
  e) 10° or 350°
  f) 45° or 315°
  g) 150° or 210°
  h) 180°

20.
  a) -45°   **b)** 0°   **c)** 45°
  d) -30°   **e)** -80° **f)** 89°
  g) 5°   **h)** 60°

Lesson Eight (pages 83–85)

1.
  a) $b = 50$ inches $\alpha = 67.4°$ $\beta = 22.6°$
  b) $\beta = 53.13°$ $b = 8$ ft. $c = 10$ ft.
  c) $c = 11.55$ cm $a = 5.77$ cm $\beta = 60°$
  d) $c = 9.43$ cm $\alpha = 58°$ $\beta = 32°$
  e) $b = 15.6$ m $\alpha = 30°$ $\beta = 60°$
  f) $\alpha = 40°$ $c = 18.3$ cm $a = 11.5$ cm
  g) $c = 58.5$ ft. $b = 55$ ft. $\alpha = 20°$
  h) $c = 11.4$ inches $\alpha = 37.9°$ $\beta = 52.1°$

2.
  a) $\cos 50° = 0.643$
  b) $\sin 50° = 0.766$

  c) $\tan -20° = -0.364$
  d) $\sin -10° = -0.174$

5.
  a) 3.429   **b)** 0.960   **c)** 0.280

6.
  a) 0.707   **b)** 0.707

Lesson Nine (pages 99–101)

1.
  a) $x = 1, x = 2$
  b) $x = 1, x = -2$
  c) $x = 1, x = -1, x = 2$
  d) $x = -2, x = 3, x = 4$
  e) $x = 3, x = 6, x = 10$
  f) $x = -2, x = -1, x = 3, x = 4$

2.
  a) $x = 1$ (double)
  b) $x = 5$ (double)
  c) $x = 3$ (double) $x = -1$ (single)

3.
  a) $x = -2$ (triple)
  b) $x = 4$ (triple)
  c) $x = 1$ (triple) $x = 5$ (single)

5.
  a) origin   **b)** y-axis
  c) not symmetric **d)** not symmetric
  e) y-axis   **f)** origin
  g) not symmetric **h)** not symmetric
  i) origin

6.
  a) y-axis   **b)** origin
  c) y-axis   **d)** origin

9.
  a) Region B is concave downward.
      Region A is concave upward.
  b) Region from A to B is concave upward.
  c) Region from A to B is concave downward.
      Region from B to C is concave upward.
  d) Region from A to almost B is concave
      downward.
      Region from B to C is concave upward.
      Region from C to D is concave downward.
      Region from D to E is concave upward.

10.
  a) A is a relative minimum point.
  b) A is an inflection point.
  c) A is a relative maximum point.
  B is an inflection point.
  C is a relative minimum point.
  d) A and E are relative maximum points.
  B and D are inflection points.
  C is a relative minimum point.

11.
  a) $x = 0$
  b) no asymptotes
  c) $x = 31$
  d) $x = 2$
  e) $x = 4, x = 3$
  f) $x = 4, x = -1$
  g) $x = 1$
  h) $x = -2$
  i) $x = -2$

16.
  a) $x = 4.33$ **b)** $x = -2.57$
  $y = 2.5$ $y = 3.06$

  c) $x = -5.64$ **d)** $x = 3.46$
  $y = -2.05$ $y = -2$

  e) $x = 1$ **f)** $x = 3.54$
  $y = 1.73$ $y = 3.54$

  g) $x = 0$ **h)** $x = 3$
  $y = 5$ $y = 0$

17.
  a) $r = 5$ **b)** $r = 6.71$
  $\theta = 36.9°$ $\theta = 63.4°$

  c) $r = 4$ **d)** $r = 7.07$
  $\theta = 0°$ $\theta = 45°$

  e) $r = 3.16$ **f)** $r = 13$
  $\theta = 161.6°$ $\theta = 202.6°$

  g) $r = 4.47$ **h)** $r = 3$
  $\theta = -26.6°$ $\theta = 90°$

Lesson Ten (pages 111–114)
1.
  a) 9, 11, 13
  b) 10, 12, 14
  c) 64, 128, 256
  d) $\frac{1}{10}, \frac{1}{12}, \frac{1}{14}$
  e) $\frac{1}{26}, \frac{1}{37}, \frac{1}{50}$
  f) 13, -15, 17

2.
  a) finite
  b) infinite
  c) finite
  d) finite
  e) infinite
  f) infinite

3.
  a) {4, 7, 10, 13}
  b) {15, 12, 7, 0}
  c) $\{1, \frac{1}{8}, \frac{1}{27}, \frac{1}{64}\}$
  d) {-1, 1, -1, 1}
  e) $\{-\frac{1}{3}, \frac{1}{9}, -\frac{1}{27}, \frac{1}{81}\}$
  f) {0, 2, 6, 12}

4.
  a) 4, 6, 8
  b) 27, 48, 75
  c) $\frac{1}{2}, \frac{3}{5}, \frac{2}{3}$
  d) $\frac{9}{4}, \frac{16}{5}, \frac{25}{6}$
  e) $\frac{1}{8}, \frac{1}{16}, \frac{1}{32}$
  f) $\frac{3}{8}, \frac{1}{4}, \frac{5}{32}$
  g) $-\frac{1}{3}, \frac{1}{4}, -\frac{1}{5}$
  h) 2, 5, 4
  i) 0.893, 0.984, 0.9984

5.
  a) -2, 1, 4, 7
  b) 1, 4, 27, 256
  c) $0, \frac{3}{2}, \frac{8}{3}, \frac{15}{4}$
  d) $0, -\frac{1}{2}, \frac{1}{2}, -\frac{3}{8}$
  e) $2, 1, \frac{4}{5}, \frac{5}{7}$
  f) $\frac{5}{2}, \frac{13}{6}, \frac{25}{12}, \frac{41}{20}$

6.
  a) 3, 6, 9, 12
  b) 2, 4, 8, 16
  c) 4, 12, 48, 240
  d) 1, -1, -1, 1
  e) $1, \frac{1}{3}, \frac{1}{12}, \frac{1}{60}$
  f) 2, 2, 2, 2

7.
  a) 0
  b) 0
  c) 0
  d) 2
  e) 2.71828... (e)
  f) 0

8.
  a) 1, 2, 3, 4
  b) 5, 9, 13, 17
  c) 5, 7, 9, 11
  d) 10, 20, 30, 40
  e) 10, 15, 20, 25
  f) 2, 6, 10, 14

9.
  a) 1, 1, 1, 1
  b) 2, 4, 8, 16
  c) 4, 8, 16, 32
  d) 10; 100; 1,000; 10,000
  e) 25; 125; 625; 3,125
  f) 8, 32, 128, 512

10.
  a) $\frac{25}{12}$ **b)** $\frac{49}{36}$ **c)** 55
  d) 30   **e)** 70   **f)** $\frac{61}{20}$

11.
  a) 25   **b)** 36   **c)** 100
  d) 164   **e)** 175   **f)** 660
  g) 1,050   **h)** 12,500

12.
  a) 15   **b)** 15   **c)** 93
  d) 6,560   **e)** 3,906   **f)** 3.996
  g) 5.98   **h)** 2.67

13.
  a) 1
  b) $a + b$
  c) $x^2 + 2xy + y^2$
  d) $a^3 + 3a^2b + 3ab^2 + b^3$
  e) $x^5 + 5x^4y + 10x^3y^2 + 10x^2y^3 + 5xy^4 + y^5$
  f) $x^6 + 6x^5y + 15x^4y^2 + 20x^3y^3 + 15x^2y^4 + 6xy^5 + y^6$
  g) $x^6 + 12x^5 + 60x^4 + 160x^3 + 240x^2 + 192x + 64$
  h) $x^6 - 12x^5 + 60x^4 - 160x^3 + 240x^2 - 192x + 64$